Anthony Stamp

Beercott

Somebody's pinched my Bottom!
A play in 2 acts

First Published in Great Britain in 2020 by Beercott Books.

Copyright: © Anthony Stamp 2020

ISBN: 978-1-9163953-2-9

Anthony Stamp has asserted his rights to be identified
as the author of this book.

Title is fully protected under copyright. All rights, including professional and amateur stage production, recitation, lecturing, public reading, motion picture, radio broadcasting, television and the rights of translation into foreign languages are strictly reserved.

A catalogue record of this book is available from the British Library.

No one shall make any changes to the play for the purpose of production. No part of this book may be reproduced, stored in a retrieval system, or transmitted in any form, by any means, now known or yet to be invented. This includes mechanical, electronic, photocopying, recording, videotaping, or otherwise, without the prior written permission of the publisher. No one shall upload this title, or part of this title, to social media websites.

Professional and amateur producers are hereby warned that title is subject to a licencing fee. Publication of this play does not imply availability for performance. Both amateurs and professionals considering a production are strongly advised to apply to the agent before starting rehearsals, advertising, or booking a theatre. A licence fee must be paid whether the title is presented for charity or gain and whether or not admission is charged.

Worldwide licence enquiries for this title should be directed to:

licencing@beercottbooks.co.uk

Title subject to availability.

---

www.beercottbooks.co.uk

Beercott

CHARACTERS

MR JENKINS – manager of Theatrical Properties Ltd, late thirties approx, smartly dressed, quickly stressed and sometimes short on temper

CAROL – Jenkins' secretary, pretty, late twenties/early thirties approx, keen but easily distracted by lengthy phone calls about her friend's outrageous love-life

MR BEAVER – fifties, Something in the City, pin-stripe suit, rolled umbrella, highly pompous and requiring a classical bust

HARRY HAWKINS – a Geezer in a loud suit, age indeterminate, a wide-boy prankster requiring a large comedy bottom

MRS BEAVER – fifties, long-suffering wife of Mr Beaver, very Country with twin-set and pearls and rather Horsey

OPHELIA BEAVER – nearly twenty-one, daughter of the aforesaid Beavers, pretty but neurotic with an inclination to wild mood-swings

ERNEST FALTER – a carpenter, age indeterminate, no sense of humour, no sense of adventure, basically a nerd

MRS GUSSETT – bombastic tally-ho chairperson of the Women's Institute, no-nonsense manner in her late seventies/early eighties

WORKMAN – is never seen, simply a voice-off, but a jobsworth with a belligerent attitude

The play is set in the outer office of Theatrical Properties Ltd, somewhere in London.
The time is the present.

ACT 1

The outer office of Theatrical Properties Ltd. It is a fairly basic room with a window in the back wall, a door to the corridor in the right-hand wall, a second door to an inner office towards the back of the left-hand wall. A reception and enquiries desk is forward of the rear wall, slightly angled to face the door to the corridor. A sign stands on the desk reading: THEATRICAL PROPERTIES LTD – ENQUIRIES. There are several cabinets with drawers against the walls, each drawer labelled: WIGS, NOSES, HATS, BOTTOMS, etc. There is an amount of theatrical paraphernalia scattered about the room.

When the curtain rises, CAROL is seated at the desk glancing through paper work. She is in her late twenties, early thirties, attractive, efficient enough but liable to get distracted. She is the receptionist and assistant. After a brief moment the telephone on the desk rings and she picks it up, answering brightly. There are to be significant pauses between Carol's replies as a voice fires questions at her from the other end of the line.

CAROL: Good morning! Theatrical Properties Ltd. How can I help you?... Yes, yes that's right, we do hire out costumes and props... No, you don't need to be a theatre company putting on a play... No, not at all. We hire out to individuals and... Yes a hire charge and a small deposit which is refunded when the costumes are returned.... Yes... No.... Yes....
(CAROL begins to look weary. She also thinks she recognises the voice talking to her. She seizes on a brief pause in the endless diatribe)
Is this Mrs Gussett, by any chance?... Yes, I thought I recognised your voice.... From our conversation last week. And the week before... What exactly did you have in mind this time, Mrs Gussett?... Uh-huh.... Mmmm.... Yes, I see... Mmmm.... Right... That should be no problem at all, Mrs Gussett. Let me just check I've got everything correct. You want eight full Amazonian costumes, with head-dresses, spears, blowpipes... Yes, and the sandal things that lace up around the shins... And face paints as well... And that's for the Womens' Institute Annual Dinner a week on Thursday... Yes, Mrs Gussett, collection Wednesday afternoon will be fine... Yes, Mrs Gussett, I've got it all written down.... Including the sandal-things that lace up around the shins,

yes.... Yes, Mrs Gussett, we'll see you a week on Wednesday... Yes, I'm sure you'll all have a lovely time. Goodbye, Mrs Gussett.

CAROL puts down the phone and stares at it.

CAROL: Just don't ask me to be the guest of honour. There's not one of you that's under eighty!

CAROL begins to fill in a form for Mrs Gussett's order when loud music erupts from somewhere outside. She gets up and goes to the window to look down into the street.
MR JENKINS enters from the right-hand door. He is possibly in his forties, smartly dressed in a suit and carrying a briefcase. He runs the business, and currently looks harassed by the loud music.

JENKINS *(voice raised over the noise)*: Good morning, Carol!

CAROL: What?

JENKINS *(louder):* Good morning!

CAROL: What?

JENKINS *(screaming):* I said good morning!

The music stops abruptly. JENKINS looks a little flustered and repeats quietly:

JENKINS: Good morning, Carol.

CAROL: Good morning, Mr Jenkins.

JENKINS: What was that dreadful row?

CAROL: Somebody going by in the street with a radio turned up full, I think.

JENKINS: Disgraceful.

CAROL: Well it's gone now.

JENKINS glances at the papers on the desk as CAROL returns to her seat.

JENKINS: Anything new?

CAROL: Mrs Gussett from the Womens' Institute.

Act 1   SOMEBODY'S PINCHED MY BOTTOM   7

JENKINS: Not another mass order for Wonder Woman costumes?

CAROL: No. Full Amazonian costumes this time. With the sandal things that lace up around the shins.

JENKINS: Blowpipes?

CAROL: Naturally. And spears.

JENKINS: Well just make sure it's all accounted for when she brings it back. We're still five pairs of fangs short from when they had their Dracula night last Halloween.

CAROL: They must be totally off their heads, the lot of them. Dressing up like that at their age! They're all well into their eighties, you know.

JENKINS: But they're good for business, Carol. So long as they bring everything back in one piece I don't care if they hire plastic fig-leaves for an Adam and Eve night at the town hall!

CAROL: Actually that's a very unpleasant thought, Mr Jenkins.

JENKINS: Yes. Yes, it is. All those wrinkles.

There is a moment's silence as they both contemplate the notion. Their expressions reflect the distaste of it. Then JENKINS pulls himself together and becomes businesslike again.

JENKINS: I shall be in my office most of this morning, Carol. I've got a lot of sorting out to do.

CAROL: Okay, Mr Jenkins.

JENKINS: Could you bring me some coffee in about ten minutes?

CAROL: Yes, Mr Jenkins. Biscuits too?

JENKINS: What sort are they?

CAROL: Crinkley Creams.

JENKINS: Crinkley?

CAROL: Creams.

JENKINS: Mrs Gussett and her fig-leaf party. I'll just have the coffee, thanks.

He turns to exit through the left hand door into his office then remembers something and turns back.

JENKINS: Oh yes! Don't forget that statue thing that's being collected this morning.

CAROL: The what?

JENKINS: The statue thing. What d'you call it? It's a - .

He mimes a head and shoulders. CAROL looks confused. JENKINS is irritated and gestures at a large box standing near another slightly smaller box near her desk.
The larger box is clearly upside down. On its base, facing upwards, is a large label reading 'Bottom'. On the visible side, but upside down, is a label reading 'This Way Up'.

JENKINS: That! Near the bottom drawer of your desk.

CAROL: Oh that?

JENKINS: Yes that. It's a – oh what's it called? Ah yes! A bust!

But his final word is obliterated by the loud music which again erupts from somewhere outside. JENKINS and CAROL stare at each other, then towards the window.

JENKINS: Oh my God! What the - !

He storms to the window and peers down. CAROL follows him halfway but doesn't want to get too close to him in this mood. Their following conversation is shouted over the racket. Neither can really hear the other's words:

CAROL: What is it?

JENKINS: What?

CAROL: What is it? Can you see?

JENKINS: What?

CAROL: Can you see where it's coming from?

JENKINS: Shut up a minute! I'm trying to see where it's coming from!

While CAROL looks slightly put out by this, JENKINS cranes his neck further at the window. Suddenly he stiffens with indignation.

JENKINS: It's a workman!

CAROL: Sorry?

JENKINS: A workman!

CAROL: A Walkman? Must be a powerful one.

JENKINS: Not a Walkman! A workman! On the pavement right below! He's got a radio!

CAROL: A Turkish man with a faded what?

JENKINS: Not a Turkish man! A workman! A workman with a radio! Come and look! Come and look!

He beckons CAROL to the window. Together they peer down into the street.

CAROL: Oh! A workman!

JENKINS: Yes. But he doesn't appear to be doing any work!

CAROL: Nice radio though!

JENKINS: Never mind his radio! It's too loud! We can't put up with this all morning! We'll never hear ourselves think!

CAROL: What did you say?

JENKINS: My point exactly!

CAROL: Well we can't really stop him, can we?

JENKINS: Oh can't we?

He goes to open the window. CAROL looks worried.

CAROL: Mr Jenkins, what are you doing?

JENKINS: I'm going to give him a piece of my mind.

CAROL: But he won't hear you.

JENKINS: He'll hear me, don't you worry!

CAROL: Now Mr Jenkins...

JENKINS: What?

CAROL: Well we don't want any unpleasantness, do we?

JENKINS: I shall be perfectly pleasant. Just firm. Firm but fair, that's my motto.

CAROL (*doubtfully*): Yes...

JENKINS: Firm but fair.

CAROL (*a last attempt*): But remember your blood pressure, Mr Jenkins.

JENKINS: There's nothing the matter with my blood pressure.

CAROL: Not at the moment, no...

JENKINS: Look! Just stand back and leave this to me.

> *CAROL retreats to her desk while JENKINS opens the window decisively. He half leans out. The music becomes louder. JENKINS addresses the workman in the street below. He is firm, terse, just on the safe side of polite.*

JENKINS: You down there! I say! You! You down there!

> *There is no reply. Just music. JENKINS leans out a little farther.*

JENKINS (*louder*): Hello! You down there! You down there with the spade and the radio! Hello! Hello!

> *Still no response.*

JENKINS (*yelling*): Down there! You! Can you hear me?

WORKMAN (*voice off*): You talking to me, mate?

JENKINS: What? Sorry?

WORKMAN (*vo*): You talking to me?

JENKINS: What? Yes, you! Yes I'm talking to you!

WORKMAN (*vo*): What?

JENKINS: I said I'm talking to you!

WORKMAN (*vo*): Can't hear you, mate!

JENKINS: What?

WORKMAN (*vo*): Can't hear you, mate! You'll have to speak up!

JENKINS: Well turn it off!

WORKMAN (*vo*): You what?

JENKINS: I said turn it off!

WORKMAN *(vo):* No good, mate. Your mouth's moving but nothing's coming out!

JENKINS: TURN IT OFF!

WORKMAN *(vo):* Hang on a minute, mate. I'll turn this off.

There is sudden blessed silence.

WORKMAN *(vo):* Now then. What d'you want?

JENKINS: What are you doing?

WORKMAN *(vo):* Working, mate.

JENKINS: Working at what?

WORKMAN *(vo):* Digging an 'ole, mate.

JENKINS: But there isn't a hole.

WORKMAN *(vo):* Not yet, there isn't. Haven't started yet. But there will be. When I start. Big 'ole. Just 'ere.

JENKINS: Well could you possibly dig it more quietly, please?

WORKMAN *(vo with sharp intake of breath):* Don't know about that, mate. Heavy work, you know. Digging an 'ole. Bound to be some subsidiary audio overspill.

JENKINS: What?

WORKMAN *(vo):* Noise, mate. Superfluous noise. Digging an 'ole. Noisy work, that is.

JENKINS: I mean the music.

WORKMAN *(vo):* What music?

JENKINS: The music that was blaring out of your radio.

WORKMAN *(vo):* I've turned that off.

JENKINS: Yes, well you have now.

WORKMAN *(vo):* Yes, well that's ambient sound, mate. To help me concentrate.

JENKINS: Well it's not helping us concentrate. We're trying to work up here.

WORKMAN *(vo):* Well I'm trying to work down here.

JENKINS: But you haven't done anything yet.

WORKMAN *(vo):* That's cos you're distracting me.

JENKINS: Well just keep the noise down, alright?

WORKMAN *(vo):* You're the one raising your voice, mate.

JENKINS: Just keep *(more quietly)* – Just keep the noise down. Please.

WORKMAN *(vo):* Whatever you say, guv. Whatever you say.

JENKINS: Thank you so much.

> *He slams the window shut, clearly flustered by the encounter, then calms himself, turning back to CAROL. He is now a little smug.*

JENKINS: There. Think I handled that rather well.

CAROL *(suppressing a smirk):* Yes, Mr Jenkins.

JENKINS: You just have to be firm with these – these hole-digging types. Let them know who's boss. They soon spot natural authority and back down.

CAROL: Yes, Mr Jenkins.

JENKINS: Now. I shall be in my office.

> *As JENKINS heads for the door left, the music blares out again, just for a few seconds. JENKINS freezes and is about to return to the window. The music stops.*

WORKMAN *(vo):* Sorry, mate. Hand slipped!

> *JENKINS draws in a deep breath, clenches his fists by his sides, bounces once on the balls of his feet, then silently goes towards his office door. He trips on the smaller of the two boxes on the floor by Carol's desk, somewhat reducing his dramatic exit, but continues into the office regardless, nose in the air, leaving the door slightly ajar. CAROL releases the snigger she has been containing with difficulty. She gets up to realign the box. It now conceals the label on the larger box which reads 'This Way Up'. The phone on her desk rings. She returns to the desk and picks it up.*

CAROL: Good morning. Theatrical Properties Ltd. How can I.... Oh Brenda! Hi!... Yes, yes I can talk. He's just gone into his office.... Last night?... Did he?... He did what?

CAROL now remains engrossed in the lengthy story Brenda is telling her over the phone. From time to time CAROL makes little noises of surprise and appreciation.

During this we begin to hear sounds coming from Jenkins' office – the odd grunt and growl. CAROL glances towards the door occasionally but remains fascinated by Brenda's love-life. The grunts and groans grow louder until suddenly there is an almighty crash and splintering sound.

JENKINS *(off):* OH NO! You bloody stupid thing!

CAROL: Just a moment, Brenda.

CAROL still has the phone to her ear as JENKINS appears from his office door. He holds the frame of a desk drawer.

JENKINS: Half of my desk has collapsed! That's all I need! Carol, call a carpenter – (*spots she is already on the phone*) – oh, you're already on the phone. Never mind. I'll do it!

He marches back into his office, leaving the door ajar. CAROL watches him go in confusion, then realises Brenda is still on the phone.

CAROL: No, Brenda, I'm still here. No I'm not sure what it was exactly. Go on with what you were saying. You'd got to where he'd put the oven glove on his – yes, that's it.... He never did!

CAROL reverts to listening intently while making the odd appreciative sound. Meanwhile JENKINS' voice can be heard coming from his office, clearly on his own phone.

JENKINS *(vo):* Hello? Hello? Is that Falter the Carpenters? It is? Good. Listen. I need help urgently. There's been a disaster. I've dropped my drawers. Yes, that's what I said. I've dropped my drawers and now my bottom's fallen out –

CAROL reacts while still listening to Brenda on the phone. During JENKINS' ensuing dialogue she wheels her typists chair gently backwards to peer into JENKINS' room.

JENKINS (*vo*): No, no I'm very serious! It's a complete disaster. My bottom's dropped, I tell you. It's gone all over the floor.... Yes, if you could please. As soon as possible. There's a horrible mess in here... What? Oh. Theatrical Properties Ltd. Yes, that's the one. You can't miss it. There's a workman right outside being very offensive.... Thank you. As soon as you can, please. Yes, thank you. Goodbye.

CAROL hastily wheels herself back behind her desk.

CAROL: No, Brenda. It was Mr Jenkins. Mid-life crisis, I think. Now go on. He'd got the rubber duck from the bathroom and...

CAROL is again immersed in Brenda's story. After a moment MR BEAVER enters through the right hand door. He is smartly dressed in a city suit, carries an umbrella, middle-aged and clearly very pompous. He exudes wealth. CAROL, turned away in her chair, does not immediately notice him. He looks around the room as if there is a bad smell in the air, hurrumphs, is still not noticed by CAROL so hurrumphs again. He picks up the enquiries sign from the desk, examines it then pointedly returns it with a bit of a bang. CAROL now spots him, but Beaver has noticed something on his shoe. With more hurrumphing he removes a white handkerchief from his top pocket and bends to wipe his shoe. Meanwhile CAROL has glanced away to end her call to Brenda.

CAROL: Sorry, Brenda. Got to go. Just at the best bit, I know. I'll call you back.

She replaces the phone, turns with a smile to BEAVER but cannot now see him as he is hidden by the desk as he bends to wipe his shoe.

CAROL: Good morning! Can I – oh!

She looks around briefly, wondering where he has gone, then hears another hurrumph from beyond the desk. She stands warily and leans over the desk just as BEAVER stands up. They come almost nose to nose. Both are briefly startled and back away.

CAROL: Hello.

BEAVER: Good morning.

CAROL: Is anything the matter?

BEAVER: Workman chappy outside. On the pavement. Drinking tea. Emptied the dregs all over my shoe.

CAROL: Oh dear.

BEAVER: Did it on purpose, I'm sure. Said he was digging a hole. No evidence of it. Looked like he was just drinking tea. Or had been.

CAROL: Oh yes. Him. We've had a spot of bother with him ourselves this morning.

BEAVER: Total wastrel. World's full of them. Ought to be shot.

CAROL: Yes. That probably would be best. Anyway. How can I help you?

BEAVER: Theatrical Properties Ltd?

CAROL: Yes, that's right.

BEAVER: Hmmm. *(He glances around again in slight distaste)* My name is Beaver.

CAROL: Is there something you'd like to hire from us, Mr Beaver? Clown costume? False nose? Amusing wig?

BEAVER: I have already had communications with you and am here as agreed to collect it.

CAROL: Oh I see. And what exactly - ?

BEAVER: It's for my lovely daughter's coming of age party. Just the thing to set the room off to perfection and lend the occasion that extra soupcon of dignity.

CAROL: Yes, I see.

BEAVER: Centre of the mantelpiece, I thought. Excellent focal-point for the room, catching the eye as the guests come in.

CAROL: Well. She's obviously a very lucky girl, your daughter.

BEAVER *(expression clouding for just a moment):* Hmmm. Yes, well. There's been some slight friction there, you know. Minor difference of opinion, d'you see?

CAROL: Really?

BEAVER: Her opinion. And her mother's and mine. Not quite eye to eye with other, if you get my meaning.

CAROL: Well yes. I think I do.

BEAVER seems to come from his thoughts. His manner is suddenly businesslike again. He hurrumphs.

BEAVER: Yes, well. That's no concern of yours, young lady. Just let me have the item as previously arranged and I'll be on my way. Busy man, you know. Other things to arrange. Can't stand around here all day indulging in idle chatter.

CAROL: I see. Well if you could just tell me what it is you're here for.

BEAVER: What?

CAROL: What exactly is it we are keeping for you?

BEAVER: Oh. Yes. With you. I'm here to collect a bust.

His final word is obliterated by the sound of a pneumatic drill in the street outside. They both look towards the window then back. Their subsequent conversation is shouted over the noise. Neither can hear the other.

CAROL: Sorry?

BEAVER: I'm here to collect a bust!

CAROL: A what?

BEAVER: A bust!

CAROL: Sorry?

BEAVER: Bust!

CAROL: A bus?

BEAVER: Bust!

CAROL: What?

BEAVER: BUST!

JENKINS storms from his office. He does not notice BEAVER.

JENKINS: Right! That does it!

CAROL: Pardon?

> *JENKINS goes to the window and wrenches it open. He leans out. The sound of the drill gets louder. BEAVER is getting frustrated.*

JENKINS (*shouting*): You down there! Turn that off! TURN IT OFF!

> *There is no change. The Workman clearly cannot hear him. JENKINS slams the window shut and marches back to stand by CAROL.*

JENKINS: This is ridiculous!

CAROL: What?

JENKINS: I've a good mind to go down there!

CAROL: What?

BEAVER: Look here - !

> *JENKINS notices BEAVER for the first time.*

JENKINS: What?

BEAVER: I want my bust!

JENKINS: What? *(to CAROL)* What did he say?

CAROL: Bus, I think.

JENKINS: What?

CAROL: Bus!

BEAVER: No! Bust!

JENKINS: Bust?

CAROL: Bust!

BEAVER: Bust!!

> *At this moment the drilling stops briefly. JENKINS has caught the last word. He looks delighted, thinking BEAVER has arrived to repair the drawer of his desk.*

JENKINS: Bust? Oh! Bust! *(to CAROL)* Bust! Bottom drawer!

CAROL: What?

JENKINS: Bottom drawer! *(to BEAVER)* This way.

As JENKINS heads back to his office the drilling starts up again. JENKINS does not realise BEAVER is not following him. BEAVER looks supremely frustrated and puce.

BEAVER *(shouting over the noise):* What is going on here? Who was that?

CAROL: What? Oh that was just Mr Jenkins.

BEAVER: The man's an idiot!

CAROL: What?

BEAVER: I said the man's an idiot!

The drilling stops again. They both look momentarily bewildered.

BEAVER: Thank God for that! Now then. I want my bust!

CAROL: Yes, of course, Mr Beaver. Now what did Mr Jenkins say? Bottom drawer?

She comes out from behind her desk, looking briefly around, then spots the drawer of the cabinet labelled 'Bottoms'. Her expression clears. She goes to it and removes a pre-packed box. BEAVER, having scowled in the direction of Jenkins' office, has now returned to stooping to wipe again at his tea-stained shoe. CAROL returns to him with the box and is holding it out to him when he straightens. He jumps back in surprise.

CAROL: Here we are, Mr Beaver. All packed and ready to go. There's just the hire fee and deposit to pay.

She places the box on the edge of her desk and finds a form and a pen. BEAVER eyes the box suspiciously as he hands over some money.

BEAVER: Not as big as I'd expected.

CAROL: Well size isn't everything, you know.

BEAVER *(sharply):* What?

CAROL: You'll have to sign for everything, you know.

BEAVER snatches the form and scrawls across it. He hands it back and picks up the box.

BEAVER: Not as heavy as I'd expected either.

CAROL: It's the new materials they use these days, I expect.

There comes another burst of drilling from outside which forestalls any further reply BEAVER might have made.

BEAVER *(shouted):* Good day!

CAROL: Goodbye, Mr Beaver! *(smiling cheerfully and confident he can't hear her)* Enjoy your bust, you pompous oaf! And don't eat it all at once!

BEAVER, who indeed has not heard, gives her a curt nod from the right hand door and exits. JENKINS comes out of his office looking around in outraged confusion.

JENKINS: Where is he?

CAROL: What?

JENKINS: I said – WHERE IS HE?

The drilling abruptly stops during his sentence, leaving JENKINS shouting in the sudden silence. He clears his throat awkwardly.

JENKINS: Where is he?

CAROL: He's just gone.

JENKINS: But he hasn't repaired my desk.

CAROL: He wasn't here to repair your desk.

JENKINS *(not listening):* I showed him the desk – what's left of it – and the drawer with the bottom fallen out. Told him not to step on the papers all over the floor and what I needed him to do. Asked him how long it would take to repair – because I'm a busy man and can't just idle away the day – and what it would cost. Thought he was quiet. Thought he was thinking the job through. Then I turned round and he wasn't there. I'd been talking to myself like an idiot!

CAROL: That's because he wasn't the repair man, Mr Jenkins. He was a customer who'd come to collect something.

JENKINS: Huh! Well he might have told me!

CAROL: You wouldn't have heard him if he had, with all that noise going on.

JENKINS: Yes. It's gone suspiciously quiet out there. Dare we hope the wretched man has finished his hole?

JENKINS slips over to the window furtively, as if the workman might notice him and start drilling again out of spite. He peers through the window.

CAROL: What's happening down there?

JENKINS: He appears to be in conversation with that chap who was just in here.

CAROL: Mr Beaver?

JENKINS: Yes. Most curious. Beaver is hopping up and down on one leg and showing the workman his shoe.

CAROL: Ah...

JENKINS: D'you suppose the fellow's entirely alright? *(He taps the side of his head)* I mean he's got our property there. Hope he's not going to damage it.

CAROL: Well at least he's paid the deposit.

JENKINS: Oh! I say!

CAROL: What's happened?

JENKINS: The workman has just emptied the contents of his mug over Beaver's other shoe.

CAROL: Oh dear.

JENKINS: Beaver's dancing about like a madman. Can't tell if it's because he's angry or because his feet are wet. Just a minute. Oh! He's shaking his fist at the workman. The workman's getting to his feet. They're squaring up.

CAROL gets to her feet to go and look.

CAROL: Is there going to be a fight?

JENKINS: Could be. Can't tell yet. Hope he doesn't drop our property.

CAROL: Mr Jenkins!

JENKINS: Oh. No, wait. Beaver's backed off. He's attempting a dignified retreat. Ah. It hasn't worked though. He's just tripped over a lady with a little dog. Workman's having a good laugh about it, the lout!

CAROL sits again.

JENKINS: Ooh!

CAROL: What is it?

JENKINS: Mr Beaver's just made an extremely rude gesture. And... ah yes. The workman's made a ruder one back. Beaver has untangled himself from the lady and her dog and is marching away down the street. Our goods remain intact.

CAROL: Workman one, Beaver nil then.

JENKINS: Pretty much.

CAROL: What about the hole the workman was digging?

JENKINS: Hard to tell. He's certainly made a right mess of the pavement. And now he's...

CAROL: What?

JENKINS *(indignant):* He's pouring out more tea from a flask. And he's started eating his sandwiches. It's not even mid morning. He can't be on a tea-break yet!

JENKINS starts to open the window. CAROL springs forward with concern.

CAROL: Mr Jenkins! What are you doing?

JENKINS: I'm going to ask him what he thinks *he's* doing. That's what!

CAROL: I don't think that's a good idea.

JENKINS: I do!

CAROL: He's gone quiet. Just leave him to it. Enjoy the peace while it lasts.

JENKINS closes the window reluctantly. CAROL gently leads him back to her desk where he sits.

JENKINS: Wasting tax-payers' money like that. What an oaf!

CAROL: Calm down, Mr Jenkins. Remember your blood pressure. You just sit there and I'll make you that nice cup of coffee. I won't be a moment.

She goes through the door left to Jenkins' office and the kitchen beyond. JENKINS glares once or twice towards the window, then becomes absorbed in some paperwork on the desk. He picks up a sheet of paper.

JENKINS *(reading)*: Order for one giraffe suit with pink Wellington boots. Eight full Amazonian costumes with blowpipes and spears... Oh. Mrs Gussett. *(He shudders and calls to Carol)* No Crinkley Cream biscuits please!

CAROL *(off)*: Okay!

JENKINS *(reading)*: Batman and Robin costumes with full accessories returned. Oh! They bent the Batarang.

CAROL *(off)*: They forfeited the deposit though.

JENKINS: That's okay then. And we can probably bend it back into shape.

He picks up another sheet of paper.

JENKINS: Now let's see. Collected... One wig selection... one Phantom of the Opera Mask... and one ornamental bust. Good!

CAROL enters from left with two coffee mugs.

CAROL: Coffee, Mr Jenkins.

JENKINS: Thank you.

CAROL hands JENKINS one mug and comes around to the front of the desk with the other. She puts it down then leans over the desk to shuffle some papers into order. Her back is to the right hand door as HARRY HAWKINS enters. He looks like a dodgy car salesman. He wears a loud suit. He leans on the door frame, grinning, as he admires CAROL'S posterior.

HAWKINS: Well hello! Have you got a bottom...!

CAROL straightens and turns indignantly.

CAROL: I beg your pardon?

Act 1   SOMEBODY'S PINCHED MY BOTTOM

HAWKINS: ...for me. Have you got a bottom for me?

JENKINS *(firmly)*: Can I help you?

HAWKINS: Hope you can, squire. Hope you can. 'arry 'awkins. How're you diddling?

HAWKINS advances towards the desk as JENKINS rises, visibly controlling his temper.

JENKINS: What can we do for you?

HAWKINS: Come to collect an order, squire.

JENKINS: Oh yes...

HAWKINS: Great fun, it'll be. I've got plans, see? Bit of a prankster, I am.

JENKINS *(consulting papers)*: Let me see...

HAWKINS: Known for it far and wide, see? This'll slay them. What a laugh! Can't wait to see their faces!

JENKINS *(unimpressed)*: Hawkins, you said?

HAWKINS: That's right. With an H. Double H in fact. H for 'arry. H for 'awkins.

JENKINS is still searching the paperwork. While he goes through names HAWKINS digs his hands in his pockets and looks at CAROL. He gives her a wink with an exaggerated twitch of the head.

JENKINS: Hancock... Hamilton... Humphries...

HAWKINS: 'awkins. With an H.

JENKINS: Hendrick... Highfield... Heywood...

HAWKINS: Try under H.

JENKINS: Heppleman... Haughton... Humplewick...

HAWKINS: 'awkins.

JENKINS: What exactly is it you've come to collect, Mr Hawkins?

HAWKINS: Ain't you got it down there, squire?

CAROL: Actually, try under A, Mr Jenkins.

JENKINS: Under a what?

CAROL: No. Try under A. Under the letter A.

JENKINS shuffles papers and looks again. His face clears.

JENKINS: Got it! We'd put you under Awkins, Mr Hawkins. Under A for Awkins.

HAWKINS: But that ain't me name.

JENKINS: No we realise that...

HAWKINS: It ain't Awkins with an A. It's 'awkins with an H.

JENKINS: Yes yes, I see that now. But on the telephone I expect... Anyway, you've come to collect -

HAWKINS *(proudly)*: One comedy bottom.

The drilling starts up again outside. JENKINS looks exhasperated.

CAROL: Tea break's over.

JENKINS: One what?

HAWKINS: Bottom!

JENKINS: What? *(to CAROL)* A what?

CAROL: I can't hear you!

JENKINS: What did you say?

HAWKINS: A bottom!

CAROL: What did he say?

HAWKINS: I said a bottom!

JENKINS: A fouton?

HAWKINS: A bottom! A comedy bottom!

During this exchange ERNEST FALTER has entered from the right hand door. He is the carpenter who has come to repair the bottom drawer. He wears overalls, carries a tool bag and is a nerd. He hesitates in the doorway, knocking gently, which of course nobody can hear. He takes a few hesitant steps into the room until CAROL notices him.

FALTER: Excuse me.

CAROL: Yes?

FALTER: I'm here about a bottom drawer.

CAROL: A what?

FALTER: A bottom drawer.

HAWKINS *(to JENKINS):* A bottom!

JENKINS: What?

HAWKINS: I'm here for a bottom!

JENKINS: I can't hear you!

HAWKINS: A bottom, mate!

CAROL *(to FALTER):* Sorry? What did you say?

FALTER: A bottom drawer!

CAROL: A what?

FALTER: A busted bottom drawer!

JENKINS notices FALTER, half catches Falter's words, notices his tool bag. His face lights up.

JENKINS: My bottom drawer! *(to CAROL)* He's here to repair my bottom drawer!

CAROL: What?

JENKINS: The busted bottom drawer! *(to HAWKINS)* Excuse me. *(to FALTER)* This way, please.

HAWKINS: Oi! What about my bottom?

JENKINS: My secretary will deal with you.

He begins to lead FALTER towards his office door. CAROL and HAWKINS stare at each other then at JENKINS.

HAWKINS: Oi!

CAROL: Mr Jenkins!

JENKINS *(to CAROL)* The busted bottom drawer!

He vanishes swiftly into his office with FALTER. CAROL faces HAWKINS helplessly, trying to make sense of what JENKINS has said.

CAROL: The busted...

HAWKINS: Oi! Where's he off to?

CAROL: The busted...

HAWKINS: Where's my stuff?

CAROL: The busted... *(her face clears)* Oh! The bust by the bottom drawer!

HAWKINS: What? 'ere! Are you 'aving a laugh with me or something?

CAROL: Don't worry, Mr Hawkins. It's all sorted!

She turns to the large box near her desk, still partially shielded by the smaller box. But the label 'Bottom' is clearly visible. She points it out to HAWKINS. His face breaks into a grin. CAROL goes to lift the box but it's extremely heavy. HAWKINS helps her lift it onto the edge of the desk. The now revealed side label 'This Way Up' upside down remains hidden to him. CAROL searches for a pen and a form while HAWKINS steadies the box with difficulty.

CAROL: Sign here!

HAWKINS: What?

CAROL: SIGN HERE!

She places the form and pen on the top of the box and steadies it while HAWKINS signs with some effort. He hands back pen and form to CAROL and takes the weight of the box. CAROL gives him a thumbs-up. HAWKINS lifts the box from the desk. The weight almost drags him to the ground, but he puts on a brave effort in front of CAROL.

HAWKINS: It's a big 'un!

CAROL: What?

HAWKINS: Still – you can't have 'em too big is what I say!

CAROL: Yes, it does look like it's going to be a fine day.

Act 1   SOMEBODY'S PINCHED MY BOTTOM   27

> *HAWKINS vaguely resembles a gorilla as he stumbles towards the right hand door, half bent forward with the weight of the box dragging his arms towards the floor. He hesitates at the door. CAROL hurries over to open it wide for him. HAWKINS can't resist a final wink and twitch of the head at her, but in his awkward position it doesn't really come off.*
> *He exits. CAROL closes the door and leans back against it with a large sigh.*
> *The drilling stops. CAROL goes over to the window and looks down just as JENKINS comes out of the office with FALTER.*

JENKINS *(to FALTER):* Eighty quid plus VAT just to repair a drawer?

FALTER: Well you're not just paying for the materials, you know, sir. You're paying for craftsmanship.

JENKINS: I don't want craftsmanship. I just want a drawer that doesn't spill it contents all over my floor!

FALTER: It's still eighty quid plus VAT either way.

JENKINS: It's daylight robbery, that's what it is! Carol!

> *She turns from the window.*

JENKINS: Pay this – craftsman – eighty quid plus VAT from petty cash, would you?

CAROL: Certainly, Mr Jenkins.

> *While CAROL deals with FALTER at the desk JENKINS has drifted to the window and is peering down. During the following dialogue CAROL will pay FALTER and thank him, then FALTER will move to the door but hesitate and start to gaze around at the various props scattered around the room.*

JENKINS: At least that dreadful drilling has stopped... He seems to have dug up half the pavement now... Hah! He's having another tea-break. No doubt exhausted himself making all that noise!... How many packets of sandwiches has he brought with him?... Hello! There's that chap we've just had in here! What an oik! What on earth is he carrying? That box is almost as big as him. He can't be able to see a thing in front of him... Oh er! He's now heading directly for the workman's hole in the pavement! Oh this should be good! Carol! Carol! Come and have a look! He's bound to go in!

CAROL goes to the window and peers out too. So does FALTER.

JENKINS: There! Look! He's heading straight for it! He can't miss! Couldn't happen to a better man! Wait for it! Any second now!

The three crane their necks at the window for a few seconds in anticipation. Then their shoulders visibly slouch.

JENKINS: He missed it! Right at the last second! How could that happen?

JENKINS and CAROL turn and realise that FALTER is stood with them. JENKINS bristles.

JENKINS: Yes? You're still here?

FALTER: Yes.

JENKINS: Well? Was there something else? Some additional hidden expense you previously overlooked perhaps?

FALTER: No. But I just noticed that you do fancy dress costumes.

JENKINS: Theatrical properties actually.

FALTER: Fancy dress costumes, yes. Well you see funnily enough I've been invited to one. A fancy dress party. Only I've never actually been to one before. I don't go to parties of any kind very much. Well never actually. Well anyway I've been invited to this one only I don't really know what to go as. But now I know you exist here I may just come back and pick your brains.

JENKINS *(unenthusiastically):* Really?

FALTER: When I'm not so busy.

JENKINS: Yes well you know where we are now.

FALTER: Oh yes, indeed I do. So I shall make a point of returning when I have a bit of a window and then I shall ask you to advise me on what to go as.

JENKINS: How about going as an expensive carpenter?

FALTER: I beg your pardon?

CAROL *(easing FALTER towards the door):* We'd love to help you.

FALTER: Oh good. Good. That's such a weight off my mind, you know. I've been worrying myself silly about how to dress up for this party for weeks.

CAROL *(at the door):* Don't you worry, Mr Falter. We'll find you something suitable.

FALTER *(with a last look around):* Oh thank you. I don't imagine you're very expensive, are you?

FALTER exits.

JENKINS: Eighty quid plus VAT per item!

CAROL: Mr Jenkins!

JENKINS: Well it's daylight robbery!

CAROL: At least you've got your desk fixed again.

JENKINS: Yes, that's true.

CAROL: And that row out there has stopped.

JENKINS: For now.

CAROL: Well maybe he's finished digging. The hole in the pavement is big enough.

JENKINS: I wouldn't bet on it. And he'll probably make just as much noise filling it in again!

CAROL: Now calm down, Mr Jenkins. We've had a bad morning so far, but everything's alright again now.

JENKINS: Yes, I don't suppose it can get any worse.

CAROL: Of course it can't. All the problems are solved.

JENKINS: Well I'll be in my office then. I've still got lots of sorting out to do.

He exits via the door left. CAROL sits at her desk and begins to shuffle papers. The phone rings. She picks it up.

CAROL: Good morning. Theatrical - . Oh Brenda! ... Yes, yes, all calm again now... We'd done the bit with the oven glove and the part with the rubber duck... Lederhosen? Yes, yes. Go on...!

While CAROL listens attentively with the odd appreciative sound, the right hand door slowly opens. A young girl slips into the room very furtively. She is OPHELIA BEAVER, the daughter of Mr Beaver and for whom the coming of age party is in honour. She is twenty-one, pretty, obviously posh, but currently looking very hounded. She is subject to alarmingly sudden mood-swings. She closes the door with exaggerated care, leans against it and breathes out. Then, alert again, she starts to look around the room.
By now CAROL has noticed her and watches curiously while she still listens on the phone.
OPHELIA steps over to the window and peers down into the street. Her manner is very furtive.

CAROL *(into the phone)*: Look, Brenda, I'm sorry, but I think I'm going to have to ring off again... I'm not really sure. I don't think it's another problem but to be honest the way things are going today I can't be too sure... Yes, the lederhosen was on and the whipped cream was waiting in the kitchen. Yes, we'll go from there. Ring me back.

CAROL replaces the phone and watches OPHELIA for a moment more. OPHELIA is still peering from the window.

CAROL: Can I help you at all?

OPHELIA turns with a start. She seems very upset, on the verge of tears or even hysterics.

OPHELIA: Oh I hope you can! I really hope you can!

CAROL: Oh good.

OPHELIA *(suddenly uncertain):* This is Theatrical Properties Ltd, isn't it?

CAROL: That's right. Did you want to hire something? A costume? A prop?

OPHELIA *(angry):* No! No I don't. That's exactly what I don't want to do. And I don't want *him* to either! D'you understand?

CAROL: Not really.

Now OPHELIA moves around the room in distress and frustration. She wrings her hands.

OPHELIA: Oh it's all so frustrating! He insists on having this great big do for me and I don't want it! I really don't want it! Because I know what it's going to be like. It happened on my eighteenth and it was frightful! So embarrassing! D'you know he even got out baby photos of me and showed them to all his friends? *His* friends, mind you. Not mine. Most of the guests were people I'd never heard of and I'm sure they didn't know who I was either. Well not until they saw pictures of me naked on a rug anyway. Then they did. Then they knew me. So embarrassing!

CAROL *(utterly confused):* Yes, I can imagine.

OPHELIA: Can you? I'm sure you can't!

CAROL: Well I...

OPHELIA: And now he's going to do it all again for my twenty-first! And I can't bear the thought of it!

CAROL: Yes. I see how that could be a problem...

OPHELIA: All I want is to be with my boyfriend. He's a bit of dope really but his heart's in the right place. And everything else, if you see what I mean? But that won't do. Oh no! He wants this big do with all the trimmings. So he can show me off. And that's all it is really. Showing me off. Showing off!

CAROL: Your boyfriend...

OPHELIA: No! My father! Pompous arse! I can't bear another of his parties. I really can't...

OPHELIA buries her face in her hands in hysterics. CAROL, still utterly confused, goes to comfort her and leads her to the chair behind her desk, sitting her down.

CAROL: It's alright. There. Sit here a moment.

OPHELIA's mood changes again, suddenly angry once more.

OPHELIA: I'll kill him! I'll kill myself! Then I'll run away with my boyfriend. Even if he is a bit of a dope.

CAROL: Yes. I think that may need a bit more thinking out.

OPHELIA: Possibly.

CAROL *(carefully):* I'm still not exactly certain what precisely it is we can do to help you on this?

> *OPHELIA has calmed down slightly. She takes out a tissue and blows her nose loudly.*

OPHELIA: Well I sneaked into his study, you see. That's how I found out what he was planning.

CAROL: Your boyfriend or your father?

OPHELIA *(angry):* My father, sod him!

CAROL *(quickly):* Yes, yes, alright. You sneaked into his study?

OPHELIA: And I found among his plans for this...this farrago of a party...a card with your name on it. Well this place anyway. Theatrical Properties Ltd. He's hiring something from you. I dread to think what it is! But whatever it is you mustn't let him have it.

CAROL: I see. Well I'm not sure if...

OPHELIA: Beaver, his name is. Charles Beaver.

CAROL: Beaver? *(she remembers him).* Oh, Beaver! The bust!

OPHELIA: What?

CAROL: Nothing.

OPHELIA: Well you've got to stop him. Say no you haven't got one, whatever it is he's asked you for.

CAROL: Well I...

OPHELIA *(pleading)*: Say they're out of stock. They don't make them any more. They've been withdrawn because of public safety! Oh please! You've got to help me! Please!

> *OPHELIA buries her head in her arms on the desk, sobbing hysterically again. CAROL hasn't a clue what to do.*

CAROL: So you're Mr Beaver's daughter?

> *OPHELIA's head whips up, hopeful again. Another mood swing.*

OPHELIA: That's right. Ophelia.

CAROL: Ophelia Beaver? That's unfortunate.

OPHELIA: I'm sorry?

CAROL *(quickly):* What about your mother? What does she think?

OPHELIA: Oh she thinks he's a pompous arse too. But she won't do anything about it.

CAROL: Ah! *That's* what I meant when I said it's unfortunate.

OPHELIA: It's not unfortunate. It's totally desperate! I'm desperate! Can't you see how desperate I am?

She starts to cry again and fumbles in her bag for another tissue. She produces only an empty packet. This makes her more upset than ever.

OPHELIA: I've run out of tissues. And my nose is running. It's going all over your desk.

CAROL: Yes. I can see that.

OPHELIA: I want to blow my nose!

CAROL: I haven't got any tissues.

OPHELIA: I want to blow my nose!!

CAROL: Alright! Alright! There's a shop next door. I'll nip down and get you some.

OPHELIA *(whimpering):* Thank you.

CAROL: You sit there.

OPHELIA: Okay. My nose has just run in your coffee cup.

CAROL: I'll be as quick as I can.

OPHELIA: Alright.

CAROL: Just sit there quietly and...and try not to breathe out.

CAROL grabs her handbag from behind the desk and hurries out through the right hand door. OPHELIA sits as if in a miserable trance for a moment. She picks up a form from the desk and blows her nose into it loudly. Then she buries her head in her arms on the desk again.

A lady enters from the right hand door. It is MRS GUSSETT of the Women's Institute, elderly and with a formidable no-nonsense air. She seems to sniff the air for a moment, getting her bearings, then sees OPHELIA head down on the desk. MRS GUSSETT snorts then marches to the desk and raps on it with her umbrella. OPHELIA looks up with surprise.

MRS GUSSETT: Come along, young lady. Wake up! What sort of example is this to set to your customers? The trouble with you young people is that you don't get enough sleep. Out enjoying yourselves until all hours then sleep it off in the day when you should be working!

OPHELIA *(nonplussed):* Sorry?

MRS GUSSETT: And so you jolly well should be! Wouldn't have happened in my day, I can assure you. Girl Guides until eight and then home and in bed asleep by nine-thirty. A good eight hours sleep, a cold wash and a hearty breakfast and we were ready for whatever the day threw at us!

OPHELIA: But...

MRS GUSSETT: But it's all fun fun fun for you young people these days. No sense of discipline, no sense of responsibility. Out until all hours at parties -

OPHELIA *(reacting badly):* Parties?

MRS GUSSETT: Parties and drinking and smoking and ... and you know what else.

OPHELIA: No I don't.

MRS GUSSETT: Yes you do, young lady. Don't make me spell it out for you. I'm talking about *(looks around, leans in)* S-E-X.

OPHELIA: You have spelt it out.

MRS GUSSETT: Yes, well sometimes one has to with your generation. And then it's not good enough because half of you can't spell! Anyway enough of this! I can't spend all day here talking to you! I was passing by on my way to M & S to take back a corset that simply isn't up to standard and I thought I'd pop in to check up about the blowpipe situation.

OPHELIA: The what?

MRS GUSSETT: The darts they fire, I mean. Do they have rubber suckers on the end? I imagine the ladies will be firing them all over the place by the end of the evening and we don't want any nasty accidents, now do we?

OPHELIA: Rubber suckers?

MRS GUSSETT: Yes. You know the sort you lick beforehand and when you fire them they stick to the wall, or someone's forehead. Great fun! But if they don't have the rubber suckers then you could easily take someone's eye out, and I can't sanction that so I'd just have to cancel the entire order and that would be most inconvenient.

OPHELIA: Would it?

MRS GUSSETT: Of course it would. Most inconvenient! Now, would you go and check please?

OPHELIA *(by now getting near the edge):* Check what?

MRS GUSSETT: Oh you silly girl! About the darts. Haven't you been listening?

OPHELIA: Yes I have been listening because I've had no choice. You've not stopped since you walked in here. And I've no idea what you're talking about.

MRS GUSSETT *(bristling):* Now don't you take that tone with me, young lady. Don't you know who I am?

OPHELIA: Haven't a clue.

MRS GUSSETT: Myrtle Gussett. Mrs. Of the Women's Institute. I placed an order for eight Amazonian costumes with full accessories not more than an hour ago. I spoke to you on the telephone. Don't you remember? Were you sleeping through the entire conversation?

OPHELIA now rises slowly to her feet. She has had enough. She places both hand on the desk. She is unusually calm. It's quite frightening.

OPHELIA: Mrs Gussett. I have no idea who you are or of what you are talking about, but I'm sure you must be a very good friend of my father. That is exactly the sort of attitude he takes with me and though I don't like it I have to accept it because he is my father. But I don't have to accept it from you. So you know what? You can take your Amazonian costumes, and your blowpipes, and your darts – without the rubber suckers – and you can stick the whole lot right up your –

The drill starts up briefly and drowns out her final word. It stops again. MRS GUSSETT is almost speechless with outrage.

MRS GUSSETT: What did you say?

OPHELIA: I said you can stick the lot up your *(drilling sound)* and then you can take a flying *(drilling sound)* at a rolling doughnut and *(drilling sound)* yourself with it at the same time!

MRS GUSSETT: Well I never did!

OPHELIA: I don't expect you have but you will next time.

MRS GUSSETT, almost bouncing with outrage, opens her mouth to speak but the drilling sound begins again. She bounces a little more then charges to the window and slams it open. Her bellowed voice almost drowns out the sound of the drill.

MRS GUSSETT: WILL YOU TURN THAT OFF?

The drill goes instantly quiet. MRS GUSSETT slams the window closed and marches to the door. She turns back for a parting shot.

MRS GUSSETT: You'll hear more about this.

OPHELIA: I can't wait.

MRS GUSSETT turns on her heel to storm out. The drill starts up just for an instant then stops, making MRS GUSSETT jump ridiculously as she exits.
OPHELIA stares after her for a moment, then crumbles. She drops back into the chair, head in her arms on the desk again. JENKINS voice is heard off from his office.

JENKINS *(off)*: I've just found a box of party accessories right at the back of the storeroom. Bit rude, I suppose, but I think they'll go well. What do you think?

JENKINS steps into the room. He has three balloons attached by a strap around his hips, two round and one long in the centre. The representation is obvious. He parades around the room for a moment. OPHELIA still has her head down on the desk. JENKINS is oblivious. He goes to the window and peers down.

JENKINS: At least that wretched workman has gone quiet again. Bit of noise from him just now but I should think he's finished for the day. Afterall it is getting on for lunchtime. Well, what d'you think, Carol...?

He turns from the window to face the desk, accessories bobbing, just as OPHELIA lifts her head. She screams and jumps up.

JENKINS/OPHELIA: Who are you?

JENKINS takes a step towards her. OPHELIA jumps back against the wall.

OPHELIA: Keep away from me!

JENKINS: I'm sorry. I thought you were my secretary.

OPHELIA: Keep away!

JENKINS: Where is she? What are you doing at her desk?

He involuntarily takes a step closer. OPHELIA shrieks again, tries to back further away but has nowhere to go.

OPHELIA: Keep away from me, you pervert!

JENKINS: Ssshhh! Keep your voice down.

OPHELIA: Keep back! Help!

JENKINS: What's the matter with you? Keep your voice down. You'll have the neighbours in... *(He looks down, suddenly remembering what he is wearing)* Oh God! Look, sorry. Sorry. I'll take it off.

JENKINS struggles with the strap. This makes the attachments wobble more threateningly.

JENKINS: It's stuck! Damn it! Could you give me a hand?

He steps nearer to OPHELIA.

OPHELIA: Keep away! Don't bring that thing any closer to me!

JENKINS: But I can't get it off.

CAROL enters from the right hand door, brandishing two boxes of tissues.

CAROL: Got them. Sorry I've been so long. There was a massive queue. I didn't expect –

She stops dead, taking in the scene: OPHELIA backed against the wall in terror, JENKINS wrestling suggestively with the attachments around his hips.

CAROL: What the hell is going on? Mr Jenkins! Really!

There is a babble of speech from both parties at once:

JENKINS: I just found this thing in the store. I didn't know she was here. I came out to show you. You weren't here but this girl was. I can't get it off. It's got stuck. She thinks I'm a pervert. I'm not. You know I'm not. Don't you. I can't get out of this.	OPHELIA: I was just sitting there at your desk and this pervert appeared and started thrusting his things at me. And after that other lady had been so rude. I thought he was going to rape me or something. It was awful!

CAROL *(shouting)*: Quiet!

There is silence. CAROL moves into the room.

CAROL: There's obviously been a major cock-up. Sorry. Unfortunate expression. A big misunderstanding. Ophelia – this is Mr Jenkins who runs this business. He's quite harmless in spite of evidence to the contrary. Mr Jenkins – this is Ophelia, Mr Beaver's daughter. She came in earlier rather upset about what her father was planning.

JENKINS: Ophelia Beaver? I can see why you're upset at him.

OPHELIA: What?

CAROL: Nothing! Never mind! Now what exactly is the problem, Mr Jenkins?

Act 1   SOMEBODY'S PINCHED MY BOTTOM   39

JENKINS: It's this stupid contraption. I put it on to show you and now it's stuck. I thought you'd be pleased.

OPHELIA: I told you he was a pervert.

JENKINS: No, no, not like that! I found a box of these in the store. I thought they'd go well for parties and so on. That's what I thought you'd be pleased about. Not...

He loses his way with an awkward glance at OPHELIA.

JENKINS: Can you get me out of it, please, Carol? The buckle has jammed somewhere.

CAROL: Alright, Mr Jenkins. But I'm sure this isn't in my job description.

JENKINS: Get me out of this thing, Carol, and I'll give you a raise.

CAROL: Another unfortunate expression, Mr Jenkins.

CAROL puts down the boxes of tissues and goes to JENKINS. She kneels down in front of him, trying to see where the problem is. OPHELIA, watching, starts to giggle at the spectacle. CAROL isn't having much success.

CAROL: I can't see what's happened here. It's really tangled up. I need another pair of hands. Ophelia, would you mind...?

OPHELIA, still giggling, goes over to help, also getting down on her knees. Together they struggle with the belt around JENKINS' hips, trying to get it free. The accessories jiggle uncompromisingly between them. CAROL starts to giggle at the situation too.
They are still in this unfortunate position when OPHELIA's mother, MRS BEAVER, arrives in the doorway – a middle-aged lady, well groomed and with a horsey air to her.

MRS BEAVER: Excuse me. Is this Theatrical Properties Ltd?

She stops dead, seeing what is going on.

MRS BEAVER: Oh my God! Ophelia!

OPHELIA: Oh my God! Mother!

The scene freezes. The central balloon from JENKINS' apparatus suddenly comes free and flies around the room with a rude splutter as the air comes out. The drilling starts up again outside.

Blackout.

CURTAIN

ACT 2

A little while later.
JENKINS is now seated at Carol's desk. He has been relieved of the unfortunate party accessory. He is on the phone. MRS GUSSETT has rung up and Jenkins is now fielding a volley of complaints.
CAROL and MRS BEAVER are trying to calm the emotional OPHELIA in Jenkins' office, though we can neither see or hear them.

JENKINS *(into the phone)*: I'm really very sorry, Mrs Gussett, if you felt a little - miffed - by our service earlier... Yes, alright, more than a little miffed. Upset then... Offended?.... Mortified?... A teeny bit angry? Ready to commit murder then. Yes. Yes, I'm really very sorry if our service this morning left you feeling ready commit murder, Mrs Gussett... Yes, yes, I agree it was most out of order, but you see... Yes, yes. You see... Yes, I understand that, but you see... Yes, yes, of course Mrs Gussett, but... *(taking advantage of a sudden drawing of breath on MRS GUSSETT'S part)* But that girl doesn't work here! She is not on our staff! She isn't one of us... Well no, no. I don't really know how she came to be manning our desk on her own in our office.... It's all a bit complicated, you see... You don't see. No, well neither do I at the moment but.... No, I can assure you it will never happen again.... Yes, I know you are an old and valued customer... What? Rubber suckers? Well I should imagine so... Well no, I couldn't say for certain off the top of my head... *(holds the phone away from his ear for a moment)* Yes, Mrs Gussett. I'll go and check right away. One moment please.

JENKINS lays the receiver on the desk and sits back with an almighty sigh. He runs his hands through his hair. He gets up and walks around the room. He goes to the window and looks down at the street. He goes back to the desk. He eyes the phone receiver warily. He takes a deep breath, sits again and picks up the receiver.

JENKINS: Mrs Gussett? Hello? Yes, I'm happy to report that all our blowpipe darts come equipped with a large rubber sucker on their end which conforms to all Health and Safety regulations and bears a British Standard mark, No.3706, into the bargain. What...? Do they stick well when you've licked them? *(an edge to his voice)* Well we'll try it out when you come round to collect them, shall we?.... *(reverting to an ultra polite tone)* I said I'm sure you'll have no complaints, Mrs Gussett.... That's right, no more complaints... I can only apologise again most sincerely, Mrs Gussett. And what?... Yes, yes of course. I'll throw in two extra Amazonian costumes completely free of charge... And all the accessories, of course.... Including the sandal things with the laces that do up around the shins, yes... My pleasure, Mrs Gussett. Yes, goodbye for now.

JENKINS puts down the phone with another massive sigh. Then his face clouds over. He looks towards his office door then gets purposefully to his feet just as CAROL, MRS BEAVER and OPHELIA emerge. CAROL and MRS BEAVER are either side of OPHELIA who has calmed down but still looks tearful. JENKINS wades straight in, wagging a finger at OPHELIA.

JENKINS: Just what did you think you were doing, sitting at our desk and insulting our customers? I've just had Mrs Gussett on the phone -

CAROL: Don't pick on her!

MRS BEAVER: Leave her alone! She's very upset!

JENKINS: *She's* upset?

MRS BEAVER: My daughter's a very sensitive girl. Don't bully her!

JENKINS: She wasn't especially sensitive with Mrs Gussett, from what I gather.

MRS BEAVER: She was defending herself, that's all.

JENKINS: Don't I know it! Mrs Gussett has been bending my ear about it for the last twenty minutes. *(to OPHELIA)* I hope you realise what you've done, young lady?

Act 2 SOMEBODY'S PINCHED MY BOTTOM 43

OPHELIA starts to crumple and buries her face in her mother's ample bosom.

CAROL: Now look what you've done!

JENKINS: Oh God!

MRS BEAVER: Stop shouting at her, you big bully! You're as bad as that awful woman!

JENKINS: I resent that!

MRS BEAVER: You've no sensitivity at all!

JENKINS opens his mouth to protest but CAROL holds up a restraining hand.

CAROL *(to Mrs Beaver):* Take her back into the office, Mrs Beaver. I'll sort this out.

JENKINS: *My* office - !

CAROL: Just take her back in for the moment, please.

MRS BEAVER starts to lead OPHELIA back through the door, with a sharp look back at JENKINS.

MRS BEAVER: Take no notice of the nasty man, dear. He's just a great big bully. And a horrible little pervert!

They disappear inside. JENKINS is speechless, mouthing soundlessly. CAROL guides him into her chair.

CAROL: Sit down, Mr Jenkins. Take some deep breaths. I know it all seems outrageous but there's a very simple explanation.

JENKINS: She just called me a pervert!

CAROL: Well you were parading around in front of her daughter with that – thing sticking up in the air.

JENKINS: I thought it was you.

CAROL: That's comforting.

JENKINS: No, I mean I found a box of those – things – in the storeroom and put it on to show you. Thought they'd be a good seller. I didn't know you'd gone out and that neurotic girl had taken your place, did I?

CAROL: Well it's sorted now. Leave her alone in your room for a bit and she'll calm down again and forget all about it.

JENKINS: But what was she doing here in the first place?

CAROL: She's Mr Beaver's daughter.

JENKINS: Who?

CAROL: The chap who collected the bust this morning.

JENKINS: The pompous oaf?

CAROL: *(glancing at the left door)* Sssshhh! Yes, that's the one.

JENKINS: Oh well that explains it. No wonder the daughter's unbalanced with that self-important twerp for a father.

CAROL: Ssshh! Sssshh! They'll hear you. Anyway she isn't unbalanced. Just highly strung. She's had a lot to put up with.

JENKINS: What about me? I've had a lot to put up with too, thanks to her. I thought Mrs Gussett was going to come down the phone and eat me up whole! I had to promise her two extra Amazonian costumes free of charge!

CAROL: Well it's sorted now.

JENKINS: I suppose so.

He gets up and moves towards the window. He glares towards his office door.

JENKINS: Complete waste of eighty quid plus VAT getting my desk fixed this morning since I can't get into my office to use it. How long are they going to be in there for?

CAROL: Just until she's calmed down again. Not long.

JENKINS: Hmmmm. *(Suddenly thinks of something)* Just a moment. *Do* they have rubber suckers on the end?

CAROL *(bewildered):* I'm sorry?

JENKINS: The darts that come with the blowpipes that come with the Amazonian costumes? That's what Mrs Gussett had come in to ask about when all this started.

CAROL: I don't know. I expect so.

Act 2   SOMEBODY'S PINCHED MY BOTTOM   45

JENKINS: I've told her they do.

CAROL: Well didn't you check?

JENKINS: Well no actually! Not with what was going on next door. She'll tear me limb from limb if she finds out I was fibbing. I even gave her the British Standard number on them!

CAROL: Don't worry. We can check them before she comes to collect them. It's not until next week so there's plenty of time. If they haven't got the rubber suckers on them I'll go out and buy some and we can stick them on together.

JENKINS smiles at her.

JENKINS: You're very good to me, you know, Carol.

CAROL: I ought to get that in writing.

A wail from OPHELIA comes from the inner office. CAROL heads for the door.

CAROL: I better see what's happening. *(and as JENKINS begins to follow)* No. You stay there. Best not make the situation any worse than it already is.

CAROL exits through the left hand door leaving JENKINS looking after her somewhat exasperated. Consequently he does not see HARRY HAWKINS enter by the right hand door and plant himself just inside the doorway. HAWKINS' usual air of unrestrained humour is noticeably absent.

HAWKINS: Oi! Somebody's pinched my bottom!

JENKINS *(turning in surprise):* I beg your pardon?

HAWKINS: Somebody's pinched my bottom!

JENKINS: Well it wasn't me, I can assure you.

HAWKINS advances further into the room. JENKINS retreats towards the desk.

HAWKINS: Where is it then?

JENKINS: Where is what?

HAWKINS: My bottom.

JENKINS: If you don't know by now…

HAWKINS: Where's my bottom?

JENKINS: You appear to be talking out of it.

HAWKINS *(another menacing step forward):* You what?

JENKINS: What exactly is the problem, Mr - ?

HAWKINS: 'awkins. 'arry 'awkins.

JENKINS: 'Awkins? *(remembering)* Oh Hawkins! Mr Hawkins, yes, of course. What exactly is the problem, Mr Hawkins?

HAWKINS: Somebody's pinched my bottom, that's what the problem is.

JENKINS: So you said just now but I really don't see how a personal issue of that nature could be any concern of ours.

HAWKINS advances again with menace. JENKINS retreats smartly behind CAROL's desk.

HAWKINS: Are you trying to be funny, squire?

JENKINS: Not at all, not at all, Mr Hawkins. I'm just trying to understand your problem.

HAWKINS: My problem, squire, is that I came here this morning to rent an item in all good faith and as previously arranged with your good self, and when I gets home and opens the box I find that the said item is not the item you said but something altogether different. So now.

JENKINS *(trying to get his head around this mouthful):* Yes, I see. Actually no I don't.

HAWKINS: I'll put it plainly, squire. Somebody's pinched my bottom.

JENKINS: I wish you wouldn't keep saying that.

HAWKINS: Well somebody has. And that somebody is you! *(with a pointy finger)*

JENKINS: Mr Hawkins. Could we perhaps just begin this again? Calmly.

HAWKINS *(to the air):* Calmly, he says! Calmly! Listen, squire,

Act 2 SOMEBODY'S PINCHED MY BOTTOM 47

I've got a massive prank resting on that bottom, and when I say massive I mean totally bleedin' gargantuan. 'arry 'awkins is known for his pranks. Reputation I got for 'em, see? People are relying on me. And without that bottom it ain't gonna work, see? Without that bottom 'arry 'awkins is gonna let people down. Without that bottom 'arry 'awkins is gonna look like an arse. And that ain't gonna happen, compredez? So where is it?

JENKINS: Did you say – a bottom?

HAWKINS: Yes, squire, yes! A bottom. A great fat comedy bottom!

JENKINS: Ah! I'm with you now. Our Mark 3 Comedy Bottom Supreme. Yes, I know the one. Always a sure winner that is. May I congratulate you on your choice? *(suddenly puzzled)* But you collected it this morning, surely?

HAWKINS: No, squire. I didn't. That's what I've been telling you.

JENKINS: Then what did you collect?

HAWKINS: Some geezer's 'ead. Massive great 'ead of some old geezer, made of stone. Weighed a bleedin' ton, it did!

JENKINS: A geezer's head?

HAWKINS: That's right. An 'ead. Not a bottom.

JENKINS: A stone head? *(light dawns)* Oh the *bust!*

HAWKINS: You what?

JENKINS glances back at his office door as the mix-up becomes clear to him. At the same moment a feeble wail from OPHELIA emanates from that direction. HAWKINS' head whips round.

HAWKINS: 'ere. What's going on in there?

JENKINS *(jumping up quickly):* Nothing. Nothing. I think I see what's happened, Mr Hawkins.

HAWKINS: Do you?

JENKINS comes around the desk and tries to gently steer HAWKINS away from the office door with a light hand around his shoulders. HAWKINS shrugs him off and still throws suspicious glances at the office door.

HAWKINS: 'ere. Mind the suit.

JENKINS *(hastily withdrawing his hand):* I'm sorry.

HAWKINS: So where's me bottom then?

JENKINS: I think there's been a simple mix-up. Nothing to worry about at all.

Another of OPHELIA's whimpers comes from the office. HAWKINS moves that way. JENKINS restrains him again.

HAWKINS: Mind the suit!

JENKINS: Sorry. Sorry.

HAWKINS *(indicating the office door):* It's not in there, is it?

JENKINS: Absolutely not. No, no, no. Not in a million years. No, what's happened is this. A gentleman came in here this morning to collect a bust -

HAWKINS *(suspiciously):* A what?

JENKINS: A bust, Mr Hawkins. The stone head. A bust we call it in the trade. And shortly afterwards you arrived to collect our Mark 3 Comedy Bottom.

HAWKINS: Yeah. But I got the stone 'ead, didn't I?

JENKINS: Exactly! Ergo facto, the other gentleman must have your comedy bottom. You see? Simple. Problem solved.

HAWKINS considers this for a moment.

HAWKINS: Where is it then?

JENKINS: What?

HAWKINS: Me bleedin' comedy bottom!

JENKINS: I've just explained. The other gentleman has it.

HAWKINS: Well that's no use to me, is it? I need it now! Me prank is tonight and I've got a lot of preparing to do. These pranks don't just happen like that, you know. There's split-second timing involved and everything. If I haven't got that comedy bottom -

JENKINS: You're going to look an arse. I know. You said.

HAWKINS: Too right, squire.

JENKINS *(after brief thought):* Well where's the bust?

HAWKINS: Eh?

JENKINS: The stone head you collected by mistake. Have you brought it back with you?

JENKINS glances around the room. There's no evidence of the bust anywhere. HAWKINS has become suddenly shadey. He edges away from JENKINS a few steps.

HAWKINS: Ah. Yes well. I was coming to that.

JENKINS: What?

HAWKINS: Well I *did* bring it back. Course I did. No use to me, was it, some old geezer's 'ead in stone?

JENKINS: And where it is?

HAWKINS: It was bleedin' heavy that 'ead, you know.

JENKINS: So you have said. And would you kindly stop swearing?

HAWKINS: I ain't bleedin' swearing! You'd bleedin' know if I was bleedin' swearing! Bleedin' 'ell! Will you listen? I'm trying to bleedin' tell you!

JENKINS: Go on.

HAWKINS: Like I said, I was bringing it back and it was blee... It weighed a ton. Me arms were killing me. I got it off the bus – had to pay an extra fare for that stone 'ead, you know – I'll be wanting that knocked off the hire charge -

JENKINS: We'll discuss that later. You got it off the bus, yes?

HAWKINS: Yeah, I got it off the bus alright. No problem there. But it's quite a stretch from the bus stop to here and me arms was dropping off. Couldn't face them steep stairs of yours up from the street without resting me arms first.

JENKINS is looking increasingly concerned as the story unfolds.

JENKINS *(slowly):* Yes?

HAWKINS: So I put it down for a moment. Just for a moment, right? To rest me arms before I lugged it up them stairs.

JENKINS: Where did you put it down?

HAWKINS *(motioning at the window):* Down there.

JENKINS: Where down there?

HAWKINS: Just by where that workman is digging his hole.

JENKINS: I see...

HAWKINS: And the funny thing was, see, I thought it was a work bench of some kind that I'd put it down on. You know they always have benches, these workmen, don't they, so I thought it'd be quite safe there for a moment while I just caught me breath. Dizzy I was from the effort of carrying that bleedin' stone 'ead. Me vision was starting to go. Come out all in a sweat, I did. Had to use me dress hanky *(indicates the garish item now crumpled in the top pocket of his garish jacket)* And I never uses that except in a dire emergency. Spoils the look of me whistle. *That* shows you how bleedin' knackered I was feeling.

JENKINS *(now expecting the worst):* Never mind that. You'd put the bust – stone head – down on the workman's bench -

HAWKINS: Only for a moment, mind.

JENKINS: Only for a moment. And when you picked it up again from the bench - ?

HAWKINS: Ah! Now! Well that's the thing, see?

JENKINS *(slowly):* Yes?

HAWKINS: Turns out it wasn't a bench after all.

JENKINS: Not a bench?

HAWKINS: Nah.

JENKINS: What was it then?

HAWKINS: It was the back end of a flatbed truck.

JENKINS: A truck?

Act 2   SOMEBODY'S PINCHED MY BOTTOM

HAWKINS: Lorry, squire. Had just delivered cement or something for that workman's hole.

JENKINS, alarmed, flashes a glance at the window.

JENKINS: And it's still there now? On the back of the lorry?

HAWKINS: I expect so.

JENKINS: Well come on! We'll go down together and bring it back here. It's a very desirable item that bust. Anybody could make off with it.

JENKINS heads for the door. HAWKINS doesn't follow.

JENKINS *(at the door)*: Well come on!

HAWKINS: No point, squire.

JENKINS: What d'you mean, no point. I tell you it's a very valuable item that bust. And I'm not carrying it all the way up those stairs on my own.

HAWKINS: It's gorn.

JENKINS: Gorn? Er –gone?

HAWKINS: Gorn.

JENKINS: Gone where?

HAWKINS: That's what I've been trying to tell you, squire. The lorry drove off. With the 'ead on the back. It's gorn.

JENKINS races back over to him, blusters, goes to the window and cranes down, then back to HAWKINS.

JENKINS: Well where's it gorn? Gone.

HAWKINS *(elaborate shrug)*: Gawd knows. Wherever that lorry's taking it, I suppose.

JENKINS *(highly flustered now)*: But this is terrible! A disaster!

HAWKINS *(philosophical)*: It's unfortunate, I'd say. Definately inconvenient. But a disaster? Nah, it's hardly what I'd call a disaster. Not a real disaster. I mean, nobody's died after all.

JENKINS *(swinging on him):* Not yet!

HAWKINS: Watch it, squire. Watch it. Don't get violent with me. Somebody's still pinched my bottom, remember.

JENKINS: And somebody's lifted my bust!

JENKINS paces around then has a thought.

JENKINS: Was it boxed?

HAWKINS: What?

JENKINS: The bust, man! The stone head! Was it still in its box?

HAWKINS: You must be joking, squire! It was heavy enough as it was, without the extra weight of the box.

JENKINS: So somewhere in London there is a flatbed lorry driving around with a highly desirable classical stone bust reclining on its rear section.

HAWKINS: If it hasn't fallen off by now.

JENKINS: Don't say things like that!

HAWKINS: Well you know what these lorry drivers are like. The way they take the corners... *(he mimes a sharply-taken corner)*

JENKINS: We've got to get it back!

HAWKINS: There's no 'we', squire. It's your stone 'ead.

JENKINS: You put it on the lorry.

HAWKINS: You gave me the wrong item in the first place.

JENKINS: Alright! Alright!

HAWKINS: And you've still got to get my bottom back!

JENKINS *(with a glance at the inner office door):* I've a feeling your bottom will turn up of its own accord before too long. Meanwhile I've got to stop that lorry.

HAWKINS: Ask the workman then.

JENKINS: What?

HAWKINS: The workman down there. He's your best bet. He'll know where the lorry's going.

JENKINS *(doubtfully eyeing the window):* Yes...

CAROL comes out of the inner office. HAWKINS eyes her appreciatively and his manner becomes instantly oily.

CAROL: Mr Jenkins? There's a lot of noise out here. Is anything the matter?

HAWKINS: Hello, darling. Somebody's pinched my bottom, you know.

CAROL: I beg you pardon?

HAWKINS: Has anybody pinched yours?

CAROL: No they haven't I'm happy to say!

HAWKINS: Perhaps I could oblige.

JENKINS puts a finger right in HAWKINS' face.

JENKINS: Shut up! You've caused enough trouble already. Now just stand there and shut up!

HAWKINS shrinks under JENKINS' maniacal expression.

CAROL: Mr Jenkins!

JENKINS hustles CAROL back towards the inner office door.

JENKINS: Never mind him. A new snag's come up.

CAROL: What?

JENKINS: The bust's gone.

CAROL: Gone where?

JENKINS: I don't know.

CAROL: Has it been stolen?

HAWKINS: Fell off the back of a lorry. Ha ha!

JENKINS *(firmly, without turning his head to look at Hawkins):* Shut up!

HAWKINS wilts.

JENKINS: *He* put it on the back of a lorry and the lorry's driven off to God knows where.

CAROL: *He* did?

JENKINS: Yes.

HAWKINS can't resist a little wave at CAROL. JENKINS still does not turn his head:

JENKINS: What did I just tell you?

HAWKINS wilts again. His bottom lip trembles. He whimpers:

HAWKINS: I just want my bottom.

CAROL *(to Jenkins):* But what was *he* doing with it?

JENKINS: There's been a mix-up. He got the bust, Beaver's got the bottom. I think.

CAROL: Ophelia will be delighted.

JENKINS: Yes well it may solve her problems but it doesn't solve ours. I've got to get that bust back before Beaver realises he's got the wrong order.

CAROL: How are you going to do that?

JENKINS: I'm going to have to ask that lout of a workman where the lorry's heading for. It was delivering cement for his hole when the catastrophe occurred.

CAROL: Be careful, Mr Jenkins. You didn't exactly make friends with him earlier, did you? Watch what you say to him.

JENKINS: I shall be discretion itself. Besides, an oik like that will have forgotten all about that earlier business by now.

CAROL: That's just the sort of thing I mean.

JENKINS: Just leave it to me. What about them in there? How much longer are they going to be here?

CAROL: Ophelia's calming down now. And if I tell her what her father has actually got for her birthday party I'm sure she'll be delighted.

JENKINS: No! Don't tell her anything about anything! Things are complicated enough as it is.

CAROL: I think they'll be ready to leave soon.

JENKINS: Well we'll have to get them out before Beaver turns up.

Act 2   SOMEBODY'S PINCHED MY BOTTOM

CAROL: Oh my God! Is he coming back?

JENKINS: As soon as he opens that box and realises the two cheeks looking up at him are on a Mark 3 Comedy Bottom and not on the dignified visage of a classical bust, he'll be back!

CAROL: Ah. I see what you mean.

JENKINS: But don't bring them out until I've got rid of Hawkins. One of his lewd remarks could set Ophelia back by months.

CAROL: Alright. I'll wait for your all clear.

CAROL goes back into the inner office. JENKINS turns back to the room and heads for HAWKINS and the window. HAWKINS flinches. JENKINS goes by him to the window.

HAWKINS: What are you doing?

JENKINS: Taking your advice. I'll ask the workman where that lorry's heading for. *(with a glance towards the inner office)* There's no need for you to stay, you know.

HAWKINS *(recovering some of his former cockiness)*: I haven't got my bottom yet.

JENKINS: Well first things first.

JENKINS opens the window and leans out to address the workman:

JENKINS *(loudly)*: I say! I say! You down there! You down there! Hello?

No response. JENKINS raises his voice a little more:

JENKINS: You down there! You! Having your sandwiches!

WORKMAN *(off)*: You talking to me?

JENKINS: Well you *are* eating sandwiches, aren't you?

WORKMAN *(off)*: What if I am? Lunch break, mate. Come back later!

JENKINS: I can't! It's an emergency.

No response. JENKINS is getting worked up. HAWKINS is enjoying the show.

JENKINS: You, man! I'm talking to you!

WORKMAN *(off)*: I've got a name you know.

JENKINS: What is it?

WORKMAN *(off)*: None of your business.

JENKINS: Well... look... There was a lorry here just now. Delivering something.

WORKMAN *(off)*: That's right, mate, there was. What's wrong? Engine too loud for you or something, was it?

JENKINS: No, no it isn't that.

WORKMAN *(off)*: You amaze me.

JENKINS: Where's it gone?

WORKMAN *(off)*: Away.

JENKINS: Yes I can see that.

WORKMAN *(off)*: What d'you ask for then?

JENKINS: I need to know where it's going.

WORKMAN *(off)*: Why?

JENKINS: Because it's carrying some vital property that belongs to me.

WORKMAN *(off – sharp intake of breath)*: Ooh. That's dodgy, mate. Very dodgy. Not sanctioned, you see. Transporting private goods on a commercial vehicle requisitioned for the purpose of delivering materials essential to the purpose of digging an 'ole? Very dodgy, mate. Could be criminal, in fact. Lucky I'm on me lunch break, mate. Not in my official capacity, as it were. I'll pretend I didn't hear what you just said.

JENKINS: I didn't put the property on the lorry.

WORKMAN *(off)*: Still your goods, mate. Makes it your responsibility, I'd say.

JENKINS: It was an accident.

WORKMAN *(off)*: Oh yeah. You would say that now.

JENKINS: Look! Never mind all this! Can you tell me where the lorry's going?

WORKMAN *(off):* Yes. I can.

JENKINS: Good.

WORKMAN *(off):* But I'm not going to.

JENKINS: Why not?

WORKMAN *(off):* Cos I'm on me lunch break, mate. And telling you the destination of that lorry wots been delivering essential materials for the job upon which I am currently engaged would be regarded as official business. And were I to do that during my lunch break I would be contravening union rules regarding the carrying out of official business during a period specifically prescribed for rest within the working day. And that could get me into serious trouble - which I'm not going to risk for a toffee-nosed git like you!

JENKINS withdraws his head from the window, visibly bristling, but controls himself with a deep breath. HAWKINS is greatly amused.

HAWKINS: Fair point, actually, squire.

JENKINS *(to HAWKINS):* Shut up!

JENKINS thrusts his head out of the window again. His tone is polite but he is clearly having difficulty keeping it that way.

JENKINS: Look, Mr - . Look, I'm just asking as one reasonable man to another. Tell me where the lorry is heading for. That's all.

WORKMAN *(off):* You trying to get me fired, or what?

JENKINS: No. No that's the very last thing I would want. I just want to know where that lorry is going. Nobody's going to know except you and me.

WORKMAN *(off):* And the rest of the street.

JENKINS: Well whisper it then.

WORKMAN *(off):* Oooh I don't know about that, mate. It's me job, you see.

JENKINS: Go on. Just between us.

WORKMAN *(off)*: I don't know.

JENKINS: Go on.

WORKMAN *(off)*: Oh. Alright then. You seem like a decent enough bloke. For a twat that is. I'll whisper it. It's going to -

JENKINS: I'm sorry. I didn't catch that.

WORKMAN *(off)*: I said it's going to - .

JENKINS: I can't hear you. Can you speak up a bit?

WORKMAN *(off)*: Not if I'm whispering I can't, can I?

JENKINS *(realising)*: You're having me on, aren't you?

HAWKINS: Actually yes, I think he is.

JENKINS: You're just having me on!

WORKMAN *(off)*: I've already told you, mate. No official business during me lunch hour.

JENKINS: Well when does your lunch hour finish?

WORKMAN *(off)*: Oh. Let's see. In exactly... twenty-five seconds from now.

JENKINS: Alright. I'll wait.

> *He withdraws his head and looks at his watch. HAWKINS is also checking his own watch. It's an extremely expensive looking example. JENKINS and HAWKINS look at each other as they count the seconds ticking by. At the appointed time HAWKINS gives JENKINS a thumbs-up.*

HAWKINS: Now.

> *JENKINS thrusts his head out of the window again.*

JENKINS: Have you finished your lunch break now?

WORKMAN *(off)*: You talking to me?

JENKINS: Yes, of course I'm talking to you! Have you finished your lunch break?

WORKMAN *(off)*: Yes, I've finished.

JENKINS: Good. So you can now discuss official business?

WORKMAN *(off)*: Always open to discussion, me.

JENKINS: Excellent. Now. Where is that lorry heading?

WORKMAN *(off – sharp intake of breath)*: Can't tell you that, mate.

JENKINS: WHAT???

WORKMAN *(off)*: Can't just shout official business about in the street like that willy-nilly, now can I? More than me job's worth, that is.

JENKINS: But you said -

WORKMAN *(off)*: I said I'd *whisper* it to you.

JENKINS: Yes but we tried that and I couldn't hear you.

WORKMAN *(off)*: You'll have to come down here then, won't you?

JENKINS: What? Down there? To you?

WORKMAN *(off)*: If you want to know where that lorry's going.

JENKINS: Oh... Oh very well. Wait there.

WORKMAN *(off)*: I'm here all afternoon, mate.

JENKINS closes the window. He seems a bit flustered at the thought of meeting the workman face to face, but squares his shoulders.

HAWKINS: Sorted?

JENKINS: He wants me to go down to him and he'll whisper it to me.

HAWKINS: Ah. Sweet.

JENKINS: And you - don't touch anything while I'm gone!

HAWKINS: I still want my bottom.

JENKINS: And you'll get it, don't worry! I won't be long.

JENKINS exits by the right hand door. Almost immediately the telephone on Carol's desk rings. HAWKINS looks at it then away, then back at it, then towards the inner office door. Nobody

>   has appeared to answer it. He goes casually over to the desk, sits on the edge and picks up the phone. The person he will be talking to is MR BEAVER in a furious temper, but we only hear HAWKINS' end of the conversation.

HAWKINS: Hello?... Yes, this is Theatrical Properties Ltd.

>   He holds the receiver away from his ear for several moments, then:

HAWKINS: Listen, squire, don't get yourself in such a paddy. You could get arrested for language like that... *(another tirade)*... You what, squire? So your name's Beaver. So what? That still don't give you the right to call me all the names under the sun, you know... *(tirade)*...You've done what? Opened up the box and found a posterior? What's that then when it's at home?...*(brief tirade)*... Oh, an arse. Well why don't you speak the Queen's English then?... *(tirade)*...You what? *(Hawkins springs off the desk, suddenly alert)* You've got a big rubber bottom instead of a...? 'ere! That's mine, that is!.. *(short tirade)*... You're bringing it back right away? About bleedin' time too, squire... *(short tirade)*... Yes, I do know who I'm talking to. Do you? No? Well sod off then, you pompous twat!

>   HAWKINS puts down the phone with a smile of deep satisfaction. He almost dusts his hands. CAROL appears in the doorway.

CAROL: Was that the telephone?

HAWKINS *(innocently):* No.

CAROL: Where's Mr Jenkins?

HAWKINS: He's gone down to the street. So that workman can whisper sweet nothings in his ear.

CAROL: What?

>   But she has lost HAWKINS' attention. OPHELIA has stepped out of the doorway looking a bit shell-shocked and HAWKINS has turned suddenly very oily again.

HAWKINS: Well hello to you, sweetheart.

Act 2   SOMEBODY'S PINCHED MY BOTTOM   61

OPHELIA *(uncertain):* Hello.

HAWKINS: Somebody's pinched my bottom, you know.

OPHELIA: Oh?

HAWKINS: Has anybody pinched yours?

OPHELIA: I -

HAWKINS: Cos I'd be more than happy to oblige.

OPHELIA's face has started to crumble as MRS BEAVER barges out of the inner office to confront HAWKINS.

HAWKINS: Oh hello. I don't suppose anyone has ever pinched yours.

MRS BEAVER: How dare you speak to my daughter in that way! Who do you think you are?

HAWKINS: 'arry 'awkins, madam. Prankster extraordinaire at your service.

MRS BEAVER: Really. *(to CAROL)* What sort of establishment are you running here, I'd like to know? You let in all kinds of riff-raff, it seems to me.

HAWKINS: 'ere! Who are you calling riff-raff?

MRS BEAVER *(now in full swing):* Be quiet, you silly little man! I'll deal with you in a minute. *(to CAROL)* Take Ophelia back inside, would you? I don't think she should be witness to this.

CAROL eases the now-whimpering OPHELIA back into the inner office. MRS BEAVER squares up to the now uncertain HAWKINS.

MRS BEAVER: Well? What have you got to say for yourself?

HAWKINS for once has very little to say. He opens his mouth but no sound comes out. He cowers slightly under the formidable glare of MRS BEAVER – a battleship in full sail. Throughout her speech she will advance on HAWKINS who in turn will back towards the right hand door.

MRS BEAVER: Well? Nothing? I thought as much. I know your type only too well. All mouth and trousers, as we used to say. Only in your case no mouth and very little in the trouser department either, if I don't miss my guess! Only too happy to prey on young defenceless girls who won't bite back. But when you come up against a real woman it's a very different story, isn't it? Prankster, you say? I can just imagine it. I expect your pranks include peeping through keyholes and watching mucky films. You're as bad as that other one, parading around the room in front of two innocent young ladies with his inflatable wedding tackle swinging hither and yon! No doubt that's what you've come here for today, isn't it? A set of inflatable genitalia?

HAWKINS *(briefly distracted):* Well actually...

MRS BEAVER: I thought so! Another feeble little pervert!

HAWKINS: No no no! That isn't what I'm here about.

MRS BEAVER: You can't fool me, you know.

HAWKINS: I just came for a bottom.

By now they are almost at the right hand door.

MRS BEAVER: Yes, so I heard! My daughter's. And then mine.

HAWKINS: Not yours, I assure you, madam.

MRS BEAVER: Get out of my sight, you disgraceful little worm!

HAWKINS: But what about my bottom?

MRS BEAVER: You'll have the toe of my brogue up it if you don't get out of my sight right now!

HAWKINS *(weighing the odds):* I'll call back later.

He exits quickly. MRS BEAVER turns back to face the room.

MRS BEAVER *(to herself)*: Prankster? Total pranker, more like. *(to the inner office)* It's alright now, my darling. I've seen the nasty little man off the premises.

OPHELIA and CAROL come from the left hand door. MRS BEAVER goes to meet them. OPHELIA still seems upset. CAROL has an arm around her until MRS BEAVER takes over.

MRS BEAVER: There, there, my darling. He's gone away now.

OPHELIA *(tearfully):* It's not him that's upsetting me, Mumkins.

MRS BEAVER: Then what is it, my precious?

OPHELIA: It's this stupid party that Father is planning! It'll be awful. I don't want it. I don't want it! Can't you stop him arranging it?

MRS BEAVER: Now you know what your father is like, my sweet. Once he gets an idea into his head...

OPHELIA: But it'll be horrible and I'll hate it!

MRS BEAVER: Yes, dear, yes. I know you will.

OPHELIA: You've got to stop him, Mumkins, you've got to!

MRS BEAVER: Well I'll try, darling, but -

OPHELIA *(smothering her mother with hugs and kisses):* Oh thank you, Mumkins! Thank you! Thank you! Thank you!

MRS BEAVER: Well I can only try, but I'm not promising anything.

OPHELIA: You'll do it, Mumkins. I know you will!

CAROL has stood a little away during this family exchange, not quite sure where to look. Now MRS BEAVER addresses her:

MRS BEAVER: This – object – that my husband has hired from you. It isn't one of those disgraceful appendages, is it?

CAROL: Appendage?

MRS BEAVER: That – *thing* – that your boss was waving around the room when I arrived earlier.

CAROL: Oh that! No I can assure you it isn't one of those.

MRS BEAVER: Well at least that's one thing less to worry about.

CAROL: You may not need to worry about it at all. It seems the item your husband ordered has been unfortunately mislaid.

MRS BEAVER: Mislaid how?

CAROL: It's probably halfway up the M1 by now.

MRS BEAVER: Oh dear. Charles isn't going to be very pleased about that. He hates his plans to be disrupted.

CAROL: Mr Jenkins is doing his best to retrieve it.

MRS BEAVER: That man! If I were you, my dear, I should start looking for employment elsewhere. I don't think he's a safe person for a young lady like yourself to be sharing an office with. Waving his appendage around in your face like that.

CAROL: He's alright really. He just gets a bit stressed.

MRS BEAVER: Middle-aged man with stress. That's the worst kind. I'd keep my distance if I were you, young lady.

At this moment JENKINS enters through the right hand door. The three women all stare at him accusingly.

JENKINS: Well I've done what I can with that oafish – *(notices their accusing stares)* – What?

OPHELIA has retreated behind her mother, who stands guard over her protectively. They back towards the inner office.

MRS BEAVER: Come away, Ophelia. Don't let him touch you.

They disappear into the inner office. JENKINS looks confused.

JENKINS: What was that all about?

CAROL *(quickly)*: Nothing. Nothing. Did you get anything sorted with that workman? Has he told you where the bust is going?

JENKINS *(moving toward the window)*: He drives a hard bargain, that man. Stubborn isn't the word. I nearly took a swing at him a couple of times, I can tell you.

CAROL: But you didn't.

JENKINS: I restrained myself. Brawling in public – it's hardly the thing to do, is it?

CAROL: But you found out where the bust is going?

JENKINS *(now at the window)*: Yes. Eventually. But I had to agree to – Oh my God!

JENKINS has looked down into the street. He goes a bit rigid.

JENKINS: It's Beaver. Heading this way. He's got the bottom!

CAROL *(alarmed):* Mr Beaver? Are you sure?

JENKINS: Of course I'm sure. I'd recognise those puce cheeks anywhere.

CAROL: On the bottom?

JENKINS: No. On Beaver! He looks furious. Like he's ready to explode!

JENKINS looks terrified. He tries to cover it up.

JENKINS: You'll have to deal with him, Carol. I'll probably take out my anger at that workman on him and lamp him one.

JENKINS heads for his office but stops dead as MRS BEAVER and OPHELIA come out.

MRS BEAVER: I think we're ready to leave now.

CAROL: You can't.

MRS BEAVER: What do you mean, we can't?

JENKINS: What do you mean, they can't?

CAROL rushes to the window and looks down into the street.

CAROL *(to MRS BEAVER):* Your husband!

MRS BEAVER: What about my husband?

CAROL: He's here!

MRS BEAVER: What?

CAROL: He's in the street right outside. He's turning this way. He's coming straight for our door!

OPHELIA: Oh Mumkins!

MRS BEAVER: He mustn't find us here. He'll be furious if he thinks we've interfered with his plans.

JENKINS: He looks pretty furious already.

MRS BEAVER: Is there a back way out of here?

CAROL: No. Just the main stairs. And you can't go that way. You'll run straight into him!

OPHELIA *(cracking up again):* Oh Mumkins! What are we going to do?

CAROL: Go through into the back store and wait there quietly. I'll deal with your husband. Mr Jenkins will go with you.

MRS BEAVER: I'm not putting my daughter's innocence at risk by going into any back store with that – that *person*!

CAROL *(glancing through the window):* Mr Beaver's out of sight. He'll be starting up the stairs!

MRS BEAVER: Which way is the store?

JENKINS: I'll show you.

CAROL: Hurry!

JENKINS, OPHELIA and MRS BEAVER bundle out by the left hand door with much bustling. CAROL takes a deep breath. She hurries to sit behind the desk and is the picture of efficiency and welcome when BEAVER explodes in though the right hand door. He is indeed very puce in the face though it is difficult to tell at first because he is carrying an enormous comedy bottom around which he can barely see. He marches straight to the desk and plonks the bottom on it. He is at boiling point.

CAROL *(with a charming smile):* Can I help you?

BEAVER: Where is he?

CAROL: Where is who, Mr Beaver?

BEAVER: That miserable stick insect who purports to be the manager of this ridiculous company!

CAROL: Ah, you must mean Mr Jenkins. He's had to step out for a few minutes. Is there something I can help you with?

BEAVER: Some days ago I placed an order for one Baroque-esque Classical Bust brackets large close brackets and today I called for the said Baroque-esque Classical Bust, which you said you had ready for me, paid the hire fee *and* the substantial deposit.

CAROL: Indeed you did, Mr Beaver. I remember your being here well.

BEAVER: Upon opening the box on my arrival home I discovered *not* a Baroque-esque Classical Bust but – *this* monstrosity!

CAROL: Oh?

BEAVER: Does this look like a classical bust to you?

CAROL *(studying it closely):* Well it's certainly not a conventional classical bust, no.

BEAVER: It is not a classical bust at all! It is a hideous travesty in the poorest of taste.

CAROL: Well, perhaps not everyone's cup of tea, I'll grant you.

BEAVER: It is a disgusting caricature of a – a posterior!

CAROL: Yes. Yes I suppose it is really.

BEAVER: I then telephoned your office to complain about the error and your so-called manager was extremely off-hand with me and frankly downright insulting.

CAROL: Oh I'm sure that's not the case, Mr Beaver. Mr Jenkins is always most polite with our clients.

BEAVER: He told me to 'sod off' and called me a 'pompous twat'.

CAROL: Surely not, Mr Beaver.

BEAVER: And repeatedly referred to me as 'squire'.

CAROL: No no, Mr Beaver. That doesn't sound like Mr Jenkins at all. You must have had a crossed line – *(suddenly putting two and two together)* – Squire, did you say?

BEAVER: Precisely.

CAROL *(realising):* As I said, it must have been a crossed line.

BEAVER: I have had to go to immense personal inconvenience to return this – object – to you. I couldn't park the Bentley closer than half a mile away, so have had to endure a number of jeers and insults as I carried this – thing – through the streets back to your offices.

CAROL: Most unfortunate.

BEAVER: Someone even called me 'arse face'.

CAROL: Most perceptive.

BEAVER: What?

CAROL: Most descriptive. Well I'm sure we can soon sort out this little mix-up.

BEAVER: I'm sure you will. Because I'm not leaving here without my bust!

CAROL: That may be a little difficult.

BEAVER: I want my bust!

CAROL: Well the thing is...it's not actually here at the moment.

BEAVER: Where is it then?

CAROL: It's a bit hard to say. Why don't you go back home, Mr Beaver, and as soon as it arrives – which I'm sure will be in no time at all – we'll give you a ring and let you know.

BEAVER: You expect me to drive all the way home and all the way back again just to collect what I should have collected in the first place? The Bentley *eats* petrol, you know!

CAROL: Not at all, Mr Beaver. We'll deliver it to you.

BEAVER: No.

CAROL: At no extra cost.

BEAVER: No.

CAROL: It could be a long wait.

BEAVER: I am not leaving here without my bust.

CAROL *(having an idea):* Ah! Wait a minute. I might have a solution.

> *BEAVER looks unconvinced as he watches CAROL go over to the cabinets and rummage through two or three drawers. Finally she finds what she is looking for and turns to display it. It is a small bust, about eight inches tall.*

CAROL: There! I knew we had one somewhere.

BEAVER: That's no good to me. I don't want a piddling little one like that.

> *CAROL rummages in the drawer again and brings out several more busts of the same height, one by one, lining them up on the cabinet.*

CAROL: Well have two of them.

BEAVER: No.

CAROL: Three?

BEAVER: No.

CAROL: Four then. Four small busts and no extra charge. A real bargain!

BEAVER: I want the large Baroque-esque Classical Bust that I specifically ordered.

CAROL examines one of the small busts more closely.

CAROL: This one is Bach. You can't get more Baroque-esque than that.

BEAVER: Don't try to get intellectual with me, young lady. I want the one I ordered. *(He gets an idea, looks around)* Or one exactly like it. Perhaps you have a second classical bust here somewhere?

CAROL: I don't think we do.

BEAVER: Surely you must have, somewhere here.

He begins to prowl around the room, then notices the door to Jenkins' office.

BEAVER: What about in there?

CAROL *(moving to intercept him):* That's just Mr Jenkins' office. There won't be a bust in there.

BEAVER: There might be. You must store all your stuff somewhere and there's no other door.

He heads determinedly for the left hand door. CAROL panics and hurries after him.

CAROL: Mr Beaver! You can't go in there!

BEAVER: Can't is not a word I recognise, young lady. Now let's see...

He exits into Jenkins' office. CAROL is in a turmoil. She raises her voice as a desperate warning to JENKINS, OPHELIA and MRS BEAVER hidden in the store room.

CAROL: But Mr Beaver! Mr Jenkins wouldn't like you to go into his office without his permission! Come out of there now!

BEAVER *(off):* Nonsense. The man's a pillock. Caused me much inconvenience today.

CAROL *(at the door):* Mr Beaver! You'll get me into serious trouble!

BEAVER *(off):* You're already in serious trouble, young lady.... Hmmm. Nothing in here.

CAROL *(relieved):* Told you.

BEAVER *(off):* Hello! There's another door in here.

CAROL *(fraught again and loud enough for the others to hear):* No, Mr Beaver! That's just a broom cupboard! And anyway it's locked!

BEAVER *(off):* No, it isn't.

CAROL: Well it isn't safe in there. The – the – the roof's falling in!

BEAVER *(off):* It's a store room. Ah! This is more like it.

CAROL *(squeezing her eyes closed):* Oh *that* door!

BEAVER *(off):* Sure to find a bust in here somewhere. I'll just find the light-switch!

As this progresses, we see first OPHELIA, then MRS BEAVER then JENKINS appear outside the window. They are clearly balancing on a very narrow outside window sill. They face the window. They shuffle very precariously across the window from left to right. CAROL has not seen them yet.

CAROL: Mr Beaver! You really shouldn't be in there you know.

BEAVER *(off):* That's better. Now I can see. Now then. Let's see what we can find.

CAROL: More than you bargained for I should imagine.

BEAVER *(off):* This place is a tip! Don't you ever tidy in here? Oh my God!

CAROL: Mr Beaver, I can explain.

Act 2   SOMEBODY'S PINCHED MY BOTTOM   71

BEAVER *(off):* It's an absolute disgrace!

CAROL: I know what it must seem like, Mr Beaver. But it's -

BEAVER *(off):* An almost full box of Inflatable Comedy Genitals! Absolutely shocking.

CAROL: Prepare yourself for a bigger shock.

CAROL turns and now sees the three figures still crabbing sideways across the window ledge. She screams. MR JENKINS waves at her then wobbles dangerously but saves himself. CAROL recovers and becomes aware of BEAVER's voice again.

BEAVER *(off):* Nothing in here even vaguely resembling a classical bust. The place is filthy. I'm covered in cobwebs.

CAROL *(quickly):* No, I've just remembered. I'm sure there *is* one in there somewhere.

BEAVER *(off):* Just a lot of tat.

CAROL: Try again. Right at the back. Behind the rack of Long John Silver Peg-Legs. I'm sure I've seen the most magnificent bust there.

BEAVER *(off):* Nonsense. I'm coming out.

CAROL: No!

She flies into the inner office to try to prevent BEAVER leaving the store room. Meanwhile the three figures are still clearly visible edging along outside the window.

CAROL *(off):* Look again, Mr Beaver. There's a bust in there somewhere, I know there is. Much bigger than the one you ordered. We keep it for very special occasions. That's why it's hidden right at the back.

BEAVER *(off):* I'm not spending another moment in that hell-hole. I'm covered in dust.

He emerges into the office closely followed by CAROL. He moves beyond the desk, his back to the window, and starts to brush himself down. He doesn't notice what is happening outside the window. CAROL hurries in front of him so that she can see the progress of the figures at the window. OPHELIA, in the lead, has almost reached the right hand end of the window. Beaver hurrumphs as he tries to dust himself off.

BEAVER: Look at this! Disgraceful! I'll be sending you a dry-cleaning bill, young lady.

CAROL: Let me help.

BEAVER: I can do it. Stop fussing.

CAROL: Here. You've missed a bit.

She dusts at his trousers, near the crotch. He slaps her hand away.

BEAVER: Do you mind!

CAROL: Ooops!

OPHELIA has now gone from view. MRS BEAVER is nearing the right hand end of the window. CAROL pulls a hair brush from her handbag.

CAROL: Let me try with this.

She scrapes away at BEAVER's suit with the hair brush. BEAVER howls.

BEAVER: I shall have you for assault as well!

CAROL: It's coming off.

BEAVER: So's the pattern of the suit! Leave me alone. I can do it.

He starts to turn towards the window. CAROL pulls him back forcefully.

CAROL: You've missed a bit. Look. Just there.

BEAVER: Where?

CAROL: Just there.

She brushes vigorously at an imaginary spot of dust on BEAVER's suit while he flinches and complains. She sneaks a glance at the window. MRS BEAVER has disappeared from sight now, leaving just JENKINS balancing precariously on the window ledge. BEAVER has had enough.

BEAVER: That's it! That's enough!

CAROL: No. There's still a lot of dust just here.

She tries to stop BEAVER turning around but fails this time.

BEAVER stares straight at JENKINS plastered against the outside of the window.

BEAVER: What the - ?

CAROL darts around him to try and block his view.

CAROL: Perhaps you'd like to consider these lovely little small busts again, Mr -

BEAVER *(mesmerised, pointing):* It's him.

CAROL: Sorry?

BEAVER: Him. Jenkins. Your boss.

CAROL: Really? I don't think so. Where?

BEAVER: Out there.

CAROL *(glancing at the window):* Oh no. That's just the window cleaner.

BEAVER: What the hell's he doing out there?

CAROL: Cleaning the windows?

BEAVER: The fellow's barking mad!

BEAVER goes towards the window. JENKINS, now realising he has been spotted, has frozen in one position. He sees BEAVER heading for the window and puts on a broad smile. He lifts one hand and executes a little wave. Then he starts to lose his balance. He teeters dangerously for a few seconds then very gracefully falls backwards out of view.

BEAVER: Oh my God!

CAROL: Mr Jenkins!

BEAVER rushes to the window. CAROL remains frozen to the spot. She is mortified.

CAROL: I can't look.

BEAVER *(craning at the window):* Good God! That was lucky!

CAROL *(fearfully):* Mr Jenkins! Is he - ?

BEAVER: Landed slap bang right in the middle of that workman's pile of wet cement.

WORKMAN *(off)*: You great steaming twat!

JENKINS *(off - weakly)*: Sorry.

> *CAROL rushes to the window and stands next to BEAVER, staring down.*

BEAVER: He's getting up.

CAROL: He's alright! Oh Mr Jenkins!

BEAVER: Suit's a bit of a mess. Going to take more than a hair brush to get all that wet cement off.

CAROL: Mr Jenkins!

> *She rushes out through the right hand door to go to JENKINS' aid. BEAVER stares after her.*

BEAVER: I say! What about my bust?

> *There's no reply. BEAVER hurrumphs to himself. He looks out of the window again. Then he looks around the room. His gaze falls on the four small busts standing on the cabinet. He ponders them for a moment, then goes over and picks one up, studying it thoughtfully.*
> *There's sudden commotion on the stairs. CAROL enters through the right hand door, helping JENKINS who is ruffled but unhurt. BEAVER watches a little awkwardly.*

CAROL: Just take it carefully, Mr Jenkins. Come and sit down.

JENKINS: Don't think I better. I'd make a terrible mess of your chair.

> *He turns round. His entire back is grey with wet cement from shoes to the top of his head.*

BEAVER *(grudgingly gentle)*: I say, old boy. Sure you're alright?

JENKINS: I'll survive.

BEAVER: Good. Good. *(awkward hurrumph)* Still want my bust, you know.

JENKINS: It's on its way.

> *MRS BEAVER and OPHELIA enter through the right hand door.*

MRS BEAVER: But he won't be collecting it.

BEAVER is utterly flabbergasted to see them.

BEAVER: My dear! Ophelia! What on earth are you two doing here?

MRS BEAVER: We were – er – just passing by when we saw this unfortunate man fall from the window.

BEAVER: Passing by?

OPHELIA: It's true, Daddikins.

MRS BEAVER *(stepping up to him firmly):* And it seems that this has all occurred because of you.

BEAVER: Me?

MRS BEAVER: You and your ridiculous obsession about poor Ophelia's twenty-first birthday party which she doesn't want anyway. This poor man was doing his best to retrieve some item which you planned to hire from him. And look what happened? Poor Mr Jenkins might have been maimed for life – or worse - if it hadn't been for that pile of wet cement. And all because you're too pigheaded to see that this silly party is all for your benefit and not Ophelia's. If you go ahead with it then you'll lose her for good, you know. And me.

MR BEAVER seems nonplussed.

BEAVER: What exactly are you saying, my dear?

MRS BEAVER: I'm saying that the party's off. Or you have it without your wife or your daughter.

BEAVER *(almost lost for words):* Oh.

MRS BEAVER: Yes. Oh. So what's it to be?

BEAVER looks around at the others who are all watching him. He moves towards OPHELIA.

BEAVER: You really don't want this party, my dear?

OPHELIA: No, Daddikins. I really don't.

BEAVER: I've got a lovely classical bust to set off the room, you know.

MRS BEAVER: Charles. It's off.

BEAVER: Oh, well. I suppose if that's what you really want...

OPHELIA throws her arms around him and kisses him.

OPHELIA: Oh Daddikins! Thank you! Thank you! Thank you!

BEAVER: Yes, yes, my dear. Alright, alright. Mind the suit.

MRS BEAVER: Come along, Charles. I think we've troubled these poor people quite enough.

The three BEAVERS start to move towards the door. BEAVER hesitates and looks back.

BEAVER: What about my hire fee? I have paid it you know.

MRS BEAVER *(sharply):* Charles!

BEAVER: Yes, my dear. Sorry. I'm coming.

MRS BEAVER and OPHELIA exit. MR BEAVER hesitates at the door and looks at the row of small busts.

BEAVER: Couldn't take one of these, I suppose? Just for old time's sake?

JENKINS: If you like.

BEAVER takes two and exits hurriedly. CAROL turns to JENKINS.

CAROL: I really think you ought to sit down, Mr Jenkins. That was a very nasty fall. You could be in shock.

JENKINS: Perhaps you're right. Just for a moment then.

He goes to sit in Carol's chair but finds he cannot bend.

JENKINS: Actually I don't think I can.

CAROL: Why not?

JENKINS: The cement has set.

He stands stiffly, arms slightly out from his sides, legs slightly apart. CAROL has to suppress a giggle.

CAROL: Oh dear, Mr Jenkins. It's not been a good day, has it?

JENKINS: Well at least we're getting our lost property back.

CAROL: What?

JENKINS: The bust. I finally managed to get that lout of a workman to see reason. He rang up the transport company and arranged for them to bring the bust back on their lorry. It should be arriving soon.

CAROL: How far had it got?

JENKINS: Milton Keynes.

CAROL: And it hadn't fallen off the back?

JENKINS: Amazingly no. It's now in the cab, next to the driver and no doubt enjoying the ride.

CAROL: But how did you get that workman to cooperate?

JENKINS: It took some doing. He drives a hard bargain. But we came to an agreement in the end.

CAROL: Agreement?

JENKINS: Yes. It wasn't entirely to my liking but –

At this moment HAWKINS' head appears warily around the door. He scans the room, sees no evidence of MRS BEAVER and comes in.

HAWKINS: Thank Gawd. That awful harridan has gone.

He spots the comedy bottom still residing on CAROL's desk and rushes over to it like a long-lost lover.

HAWKINS: Me bottom!

He picks it up and kisses it on both cheeks, then hugs it to him.

HAWKINS: Me bottom! Oh you don't know how good this makes me feel. I've got a warm tingly glow in me insides!

JENKINS: It's a Mark 3 Comedy Bottom, Mr Hawkins, not a long-lost lover.

HAWKINS: It's a long-lost lover to me. *(he kisses it again and then notices Jenkins' awkward stance)* 'ere. Are you alright, squire?

JENKINS: Ah well, you see -

CAROL: He's fine. What do you think of our new line, Mr Hawkins? The Hilarious Stiff Suit. It would make a great prank to add to your repertoire.

HAWKINS *(eyeing Jenkins approvingly):* Yeah. Tastey, that. I can see great potential there.

CAROL: We could arrange for you to have one just like it right now if you like.

She goes towards the window. JENKINS creaks forwards with difficulty to stop her.

JENKINS: Carol, no.

CAROL: What do you think, Mr Hawkins?

HAWKINS: Tempting. Love the movement.

CAROL: Just step this way, then. *(starting to open the window)*

JENKINS *(concerned):* No, Carol. I don't think Mr Hawkins wants one these today. After all he's got his bottom now.

HAWKINS: Maybe you're right, squire. One prank at a time is enough. Always leave 'em wanting more, eh? But I'll definitely bear it in mind for the future.

CAROL: Any time, Mr Hawkins.

HAWKINS moves towards the right hand door, still hugging his comedy bottom.

HAWKINS: Well, best be on me way then. Got a lot of preparation to do. Pranks don't just organise themselves, you know. Been a few cock-ups today, but we got there in the end.

JENKINS: Hope it goes well for you.

HAWKINS: Thank you, squire. Very decent of you.

CAROL: Goodbye, Mr Hawkins.

HAWKINS: Ta-ta! *(to the bottom)* Oh you lovely beast!

He gives it another big kiss and exits through the right hand door. JENKINS creaks stiffly towards CAROL.

JENKINS: Were you really going to push him through the window into that wet cement?

CAROL: It's clearly not so wet now, is it? And yes I was.

JENKINS: A bit harsh, isn't it? I mean I know the man's a total oik but even so...

CAROL: D'you know he pretended to be you on the telephone when Beaver rang up earlier? Called him all the names under the sun apparently.

JENKINS: What? The cheeky sod! I'll have him. Oi! Hawkins! Come back here!

JENKINS starts to head for the right hand door but he can now only move in a slow stiff-legged hobble.

CAROL: I don't think you'll catch him just at the moment.

JENKINS: You're right. Forget it. Let him go. What's the point?

CAROL: You'd only do something you'd later regret.

JENKINS: Yes. Then I suppose I'd be arrested for being a *hardened* criminal.

They look at each other and start to chuckle. Then JENKINS winces at the stiffened clothes.

CAROL: I wish you could sit down.

JENKINS: Impossible, I'm afraid.

CAROL: Perhaps you could lie down? Let's see. If we –

She starts to manhandle JENKINS but he stops her. He lurches over to the desk, turns awkwardly so that it is behind him then very carefully eases himself back so that he is rested at a slight angle against its front.

JENKINS: I'll just prop here. I'll be very comfortable.

CAROL: Now about that workman. You never did tell me. How did you get him to do what you wanted?

JENKINS: Well I had to –

He stops, staring at the right hand door. ERNEST FALTER has entered and is hovering just inside the room. He now wears casual clothes which, of course, are not casual at all. CAROL turns to look at him.

FALTER: Er – hello. Remember me? Ernest Falter. I repaired your desk earlier today.

JENKINS: I remember. Eighty quid plus VAT. How could I forget?

CAROL: Can we help you, Mr Falter?

FALTER takes a few hesitant steps into the room, looking around nervously.

FALTER: You might also remember I told you I had been invited to a fancy dress party and that I had no idea what to go as. I promised to come back here when I had a suitable window, and you promised to help me choose something. Well I have a suitable window now.

JENKINS *(creaking stiffly, with an impatient glance at the window):* We have a suitable window too, Mr Falter. It would suit you – right down to the ground!

FALTER: Oh that sounds very promising, I must say. *(noticing Jenkins' stiffened position)* Are you alright? You look a bit -

CAROL: Inflexible?

FALTER: Yes. That's it. That's just the word!

JENKINS *(losing patience, trying to heave off the desk):* I'll show you how inflexible I can be!

CAROL pushes him back with a gentle touch of the hand. JENKINS tilts back to his original position. CAROL steps towards FALTER helpfully.

CAROL: Now, Mr Falter. Let's have a think, shall we? I'm sure we must have something that would –

There is sudden commotion on the stairs accompanied by several banshee-like howls. A moment later, MRS GUSSETT bursts in through the right hand door. She is dressed in full Amazonian costume, including head dress, spear, blowpipe and the famous sandals that lace up around the shins. The costume is obviously home-made. She is made up fiercely. JENKINS, CAROL and FALTER just stare in amazement. As the scene progresses JENKINS and CAROL will become increasingly nervous. FALTER's expression will take on a look of fascination and awe.

MRS GUSSETT: Stick 'em up!

She raises the blowpipe to her mouth. CAROL puts her hands up. JENKINS tries but of course cannot manage it.

JENKINS: I don't think I can.

MRS GUSSETT looses a dart from her blowpipe with a fearsome phut of breath. It shoots across the room and sticks to the wall behind the desk by its rubber sucker.

MRS GUSSETT: There! That's what you *call* a dart with a rubber sucker!

JENKINS: Mrs Gussett! Please! Are you mad?

MRS GUSSETT *(advancing slightly in warrior fashion):* I must have been to trust a cowboy outfit like you!

FALTER: A Cowboy Outfit? Now there's a thought.

JENKINS: But... but what are doing here?

MRS GUSSETT: I'm doing what I should have done years ago. Going solo. Making my own costumes. *(she parades briefly)* Well? What d'you think?

CAROL: Awesome.

JENKINS: Never seen anything like it.

MRS GUSSETT: Impressive, eh? You won't forget this in a hurry.

JENKINS: It'll be etched into my mind for the rest of my life, I'm sure.

MRS GUSSETT: So the order's cancelled. I shall no longer be requiring your ten Amazonian costumes for the Women's Institute Annual Dinner.

JENKINS: Eight costumes, surely?

MRS GUSSETT: Ten including the two free ones you offered me earlier. I shall be making them myself from now on. And I shall require back the hire fee I paid in advance. *And* a hefty compensation fee for the inconvenience.

JENKINS: I don't know about that.

MRS GUSSETT hastily loads another rubber-suckered dart into her blowpipe. She raises the blowpipe to her mouth.

JENKINS: Alright alright! Carol. Get the petty cash box!

The blowpipe is lowered. CAROL hurries around the desk and rummages in a drawer. She pulls out some money, takes it to MRS GUSSETT and hands over several notes. MRS GUSSETT counts it carefully. During this FALTER is gazing at MRS GUSSETT with great fascination.

MRS GUSSETT: This is just the hire fee. What about the compensation?

JENKINS: How about two busts? Small but perfectly formed. *(nods at the remaining busts on the cabinet)*

MRS GUSSETT *(swelling her chest):* I already have a bust that I'm perfectly satisfied with, thank you.

CAROL *(to Jenkins):* Mr Jenkins?

JENKINS *(resigned):* Alright. Go on.

CAROL hands over the rest of the money. MRS GUSSETT rifles it triumphantly and stows it away.

MRS GUSSETT: Thank you! And that, I believe, concludes our business. For ever

JENKINS *(through gritted teeth)*: It's been a pleasure, Mrs Gussett.

MRS GUSSETT turns to leave. FALTER steps forward hesitantly.

FALTER: Erm – excuse me?

MRS GUSSETT *(as if addressing a worm):* Yes?

FALTER: Well I came here to look for a fancy dress costume, you see. I didn't know what to have. But I have to say that costume of yours is most handsome. I think it's solved my problem. Do you think you could possibly make one for me too?

MRS GUSSETT regards him for a moment then her face brightens with an idea.

MRS GUSSETT: Make one for you? Of course I can! You can be our male sacrifice at the annual dinner! Tally-Ho!

She slaps him heartily on the back and sweeps him out of the room by the right hand door.

JENKINS: I'll never eat Crinkley Creams again.

CAROL: I think I'm going to be sick.

JENKINS: At least most of our problems have been solved. And, my God, there have been enough of them today!

CAROL: Except for the bust.

JENKINS: The bust?

CAROL: The Baroque-esque Classical Bust that went to Milton Keynes.

JENKINS: I'd forgotten about that. But if all goes to plan it should be arriving back any time now.

On cue the WORKMAN's voice is heard bellowing up from the street outside.

WORKMAN *(off)*: Oi! Oi, mate! You up there! Can you hear me?

JENKINS: Right on cue.

He struggles off the desk and lumbers awkwardly to the window, opens it and tries his best to lean out. He cracks his head several times before the manoeuvre is accomplished.

WORKMAN *(off)*: You up there! Are you there, mate?

JENKINS: Yes, I'm here.

WORKMAN *(off)*: I've got your stone 'ead!

CAROL: Has he?

JENKINS *(to CAROL)*: Yes! He has! *(to WORKMAN)* That's wonderful! Hang on there. I'll be right – my secretary will be right down.

WORKMAN *(off)*: No worries, mate! I'll bring it up to you.

JENKINS withdraws from the window with difficulty. He looks delighted.

JENKINS: Well well! This is a turn up. We've reunited the Beavers. Hawkins has got his beloved bottom. We've seen the last of the fearsome Mrs Gussett. Falter's costume problem is solved –

CAROL: Though I think he might have some other problems quite soon.

JENKINS: Granted. And we're about to get our classical bust back. All in all, I think we can say that it's been a rather successful day.

There is a sudden commotion from the direction of the stairs. A scuffle, falling, the loud smash of something made of plaster.

WORKMAN *(off)*: Bugger!

CAROL and JENKINS look at each other.

JENKINS *(calling)*: Are you alright down there?

WORKMAN *(off)*: You know that bust, mate?

JENKINS *(slowly)*: Yes?

WORKMAN *(off)*: It's bust.

JENKINS starts to move but can't. CAROL hurries out of the right hand door to the stairs. JENKINS listens tersely to the brief conversation.

CAROL *(off)*: Are you alright? What happened?

WORKMAN *(off)*: Tripped on the stairs, love. This thing weighs a ton. Well it did. Not so heavy now though, is it?

CAROL *(off)*: Oh dear! What a mess. There's bits of bust everywhere!

WORKMAN *(off)*: That's a nose, I think. And over there's his ear.

CAROL *(off)*: What's Mr Jenkins going to say?

WORKMAN *(off)*: Not much he can say. Not after what he did to my pile of wet cement.

CAROL *(off)*: I hope *he* sees it that way.

WORKMAN *(off)*: Well I did what he asked me anyway. Got his stone 'ead back for him. You better tell him not to forget *his* end of the bargain.

CAROL *(off – doubtfully)*: Yes. I'll tell him.

WORKMAN *(off)*: Think you're gonna need a dustpan and brush, love. Ta-ta!

A moment later, CAROL re-enters through the right hand door. She carries a plaster nose and a plaster ear, all that's left of the classical bust. She looks very wary.

CAROL: Mr Jenkins. There's been a bit of an accident.

JENKINS: I heard.

CAROL: There's classical bust all over the stairs.

Surprisingly JENKINS grins.

JENKINS: Well who cares? It was only an old bust. We hadn't rented it out for years. And there are worse things in life than a busted bust you know, Carol.

CAROL *(relieved):* I'm glad you can be so philosophical about it, Mr Jenkins.

JENKINS: I think I'm just beyond caring.

CAROL starts to turn away then remembers something and turns back.

CAROL: Oh yes. That workman said to remind you that you still have to keep your end of the bargain.

JENKINS: Ah.

CAROL: What exactly did you agree to, Mr Jenkins?

Exactly on cue loud music blares out from the street below. JENKINS winces. CAROL puts her hands to her ears.

JENKINS *(shouting):* From now on we shall have music while we work!

CAROL *(shouting):* What did you say?

JENKINS *(shouting):* Music while we work!

CAROL *(shouting):* I can't hear you!

The phone rings.

JENKINS *(shouting really loudly):* Is that the phone?

CAROL *(shouting really loudly):* What?

JENKINS *(pointing):* The phone!

CAROL cocks an ear then picks up the receiver.

CAROL: Theatrical Properties – what? Oh Brenda! Hi... Bit of background noise here. Just a minute! *(Sits at her desk with one finger in her ear)* That's better... You'd got to where he was about to push the enormous... That's right!... He didn't!... Seriously? Yes, go on...

JENKINS stares in disbelief first at CAROL nattering on the phone, then at the window. Now he almost addresses the audience:

JENKINS: I'm stuck between a rock band –

He tries to move, winces, and feels around the seat of his trousers.

JENKINS: - and a hard place. Time to go home!

Slowly and awkwardly JENKINS hobbles out of the door as CAROL continues to natter on the phone and the music continues to blare.

The lights fade to black.

CURTAIN

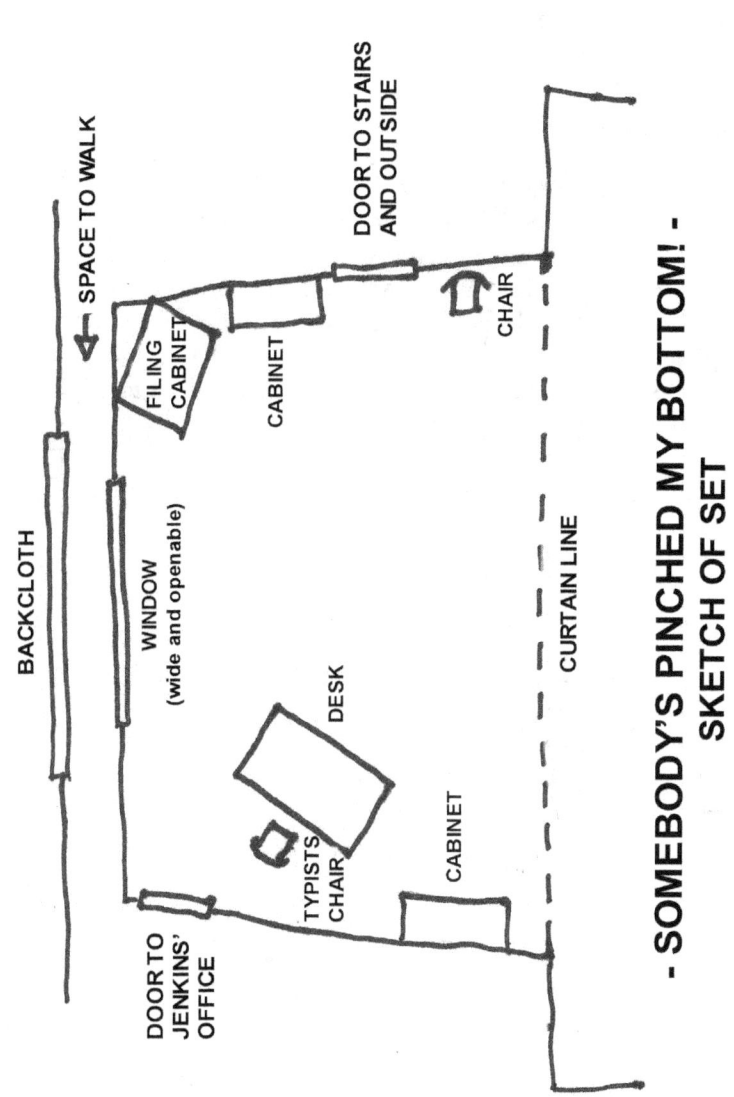

FURNITURE AND PROPERTIES

Desk
Typist's chair on wheels
Standard wooden chair
Filing cabinet
Cabinets with drawers x2
Cardboard box (large – labelled 'This Way Up' and 'Bottom')
Cardboard box (smaller)
Cardboard box (supposedly containing the comedy bottom)
Miscellaneous cardboard boxes
Miscellaneous theatrical props scattered around the set
Wall decorations – calendar, notices, etc
Telephone
Stand-up sign for desk labelled 'Theatrical Properties Ltd'
Papers (including hire agreement forms), stationery, etc, on desk

Appendix   SOMEBODY'S PINCHED MY BOTTOM

PERSONAL AND SPECIFIC PROPS
ACT 1

Handbag containing hairbrush (Carol)
Briefcase (Jenkins)
Frame of desk drawer – no bottom in it
Rolled umbrella, black (Beaver)
White pocket handkerchief (Beaver)
Paper money (Beaver)
Coffee mugs x2
Tool bag (Falter)
Handbag containing one tissue, empty tissue packet (Ophelia)
Umbrella (Mrs Gussett)
Inflatable Comedy Genitals attached to belt or waist strap - *two round balloons, one long balloon – long balloon should be detachable and should go down when released*
Tissue boxes x2
Handbag (Mrs Beaver)
Garishly coloured handkerchief (Hawkins)

ACT 2

Watch – ordinary (Jenkins)
Watch – big and flashy (Hawkins)
Large Comedy Bottom
Small busts x4
Smaller busts x2
Suit – grey with cement down entire back (Jenkins)
Amazonian costume, including -
  head-dress, spear, blowpipe, blowpipe darts with rubber suckers x2
Cash box containing paper money (Carol's desk)
Plaster ear and plaster nose from broken bust (life-size)

Appendix   SOMEBODY'S PINCHED MY BOTTOM   v

SOUND EFFECTS PLOT

ACT 1:

Cue 1: Run-in music

Cue 2: Carol looks through paperwork (p.5) - Telephone rings

Cue 3: After Carol finishes phone call (p.6) - Loud music

Cue 4: Jenkins 'I said good morning' (p.6) - Loud music stops as he begins to speak

Cue 5: Jenkins 'Ah yes! A bust!' (p.8) - Loud music starts as he finishes speaking

Cue 6: Workman 'I'll turn this off' (p.11) - Loud music stops

Cue 7: Jenkins 'I shall be in my office' (p.12) - Two-second burst of Loud Music as Jenkins heads for office

Cue 8: Carol realigns boxes on floor (p.12) - Telephone rings

Cue 9: Jenkins grunts and groans unseen (p.13) - Loud crash and splintering as of a desk collapsing

Cue 10: Beaver 'I'm here to collect a bust' (p.16) - Pneumatic drill starts as he finishes sentence

Cue 11: Beaver 'Bust!' (p.17) - Drill stops

Cue 12: Jenkins heads back to his office (p.18) - Drill starts

Cue 13: Beaver 'The man's an idiot!' (p.18) - Drill stops

Cue 14: Carol '...materials they use these days, I expect' (p.19) - Drill starts

Cue 15: Jenkins 'I said – ' (p.19) - Drill stops

Cue 16: Hawkins 'One comedy bottom' (p.24) - Drill starts

Cue 17: Hawkins exits. Carol leans against door with sigh (p.27) - Drill stops

Cue 18: Carol sits at desk and shuffles papers (p.29) - Telephone rings

Cue 19-21: Short bursts of drill drown Ophelia's individual words (p.36) - Drill starts/drill stops (see script)

Cue 22: Mrs Gussett begins to exit (p.36) - One-second drill sound

Cue 23: Balloon flies off (p,40) - Drill starts

Cue 24: Fade to black and curtain (p.40) - Drill fades out/play-out music

ACT 2

Cue 1: Play-in music (p.41)

Cue 2: Jenkins exits (p.59) - Telephone rings

Cue 3: Jenkins '...a rather successful day' (p.84) - Loud smash of something made of plaster

Cue 4: Carol 'What exactly did you agree to Mr Jenkins?' (p.85) - Loud music

Cue 5: Fade to black (p.86) - Loud music fades out

Cue 6: Curtain (p.86) - Play-out music

LIGHTING PLOT

Standard lighting: fade up at the start of each act, fade down at the end of each act

About the Author

Anthony began writing stories and books when he was about fourteen. Throughout his teens, twenties and early thirties he entertained himself by writing thirty-seven novels and collections of short stories. None of these were ever published. He sent one to a publisher but it was instantly rejected. He did however win several story competitions during the early 80's, including one of five runners-up prizes in The Mail on Sunday's very first 'Start of a Novel' competition.

In the late 80s he bought an early camcorder and, having always been fascinated by cinema and the film making process, he collected together a group of friends and made a short amateur film. Anthony based the screenplay on a short story he had written some time before (and which had actually been read on BBC Radio). More friends became interested and more films were made, totalling thirty between 1988 and 2015. In each case he would write the screenplay, produce, direct, edit and often appear in these films. None were ever publicly shown and were never intended to be: they were screened privately for the cast and friends and relatives.

By 2005 many of the participants had moved on and with a slight change of direction in mind Anthony joined a local amateur theatre group. He loved the experience instantly and, joining a second company in 2007, began performing in five or six plays a year. He has now appeared in about sixty plays and continues to do so. Anthony has also directed five plays.

Ironically his fellow actors learned of the earlier films he had made and expressed a great desire to appear in one. So he made three more films between 2011 and 2015, now with the actors from the theatre companies. The last of these was a ghost story called The Grey Mist... Early in 2016 one of his theatre companies began to consider putting on a ghost play in October for the Halloween period and, having failed to find one that was both suitable and available, asked Anthony if he could write one specifically for them. He told them the story was already written and adapted The Grey Mist for the stage. In fact the play was not performed until October of the following year. It was his first attempt at writing a stage play though clearly not his first attempt at writing.

Also by Anthony Stamp:

The Grey Mist: A Ghost Story

ISBN: 978-1-9997429-4-2

When Dr Trent takes over the medical practice in a remote country area of 1920s England he finds the locals both suspicious and superstitious. They speak in hushed tones of a grey mist which descends without warning and with deadly consequence. He believes this is only natural in a rural area barely touched by the twentieth century.

But soon he senses something more. Why does he feel the presence of a patient he cannot see? Who is the young lady who waits outside the practice but never comes in? And what exactly is the grey mist, so often whispered about but never explained?

www.ingramcontent.com/pod-product-compliance
Lightning Source LLC
Chambersburg PA
CBHW071023080526
44587CB00015B/2470